The Free Press

To the GoldBug, in thanks for continued loyalty, friendship, and support. On your journey to Catholic Distributism, we wish you Godspeed!

The Free Press

by
Hilaire Belloc

Norfolk, VA
2002

The Free Press.

Copyright © 2002 IHS Press.

First published in 1918 by George Allen & Unwin, Ltd.
Preface, footnotes, typesetting, layout, and cover design
copyright 2002 IHS Press.
All rights reserved.

ISBN: 0-9714894-1-6

Library of Congress Cataloging-in-Publication Data

Belloc, Hilaire, 1870-1953.
　The free press / by Hilaire Belloc.
　　p. cm.
　Originally published: London : Allen & Unwin, 1918.
　ISBN 0-9714894-1-6 (alk. paper)
　　1. Journalism--Corrupt practices. 2. Freedom of the press. I. Title

PN4888.C6 B4 2002
323.44'5--dc21

2002019963

Printed in the United States of America.

This edition has largely preserved the spelling, punctuation, and
formatting of Belloc's original 1918 edition.

IHS Press is the only publisher dedicated exclusively
to the Social Teachings of the Catholic Church.
For information on current or future titles, contact:

IHS Press
222 W. 21st St., Suite F-122
Norfolk, VA 23517
USA

Table of Contents

	PAGE
Preface	7
Dedication	23
The Free Press	27

Preface

> *"Left, right and center, people by the tens of millions have stopped watching network news. And that may be a healthy thing if it betokens skepticism, disbelief and an effort to find out for one's self."*
> —Nicholas von Hoffman

One of the truly remarkable qualities of Hilaire Belloc is that he subjected almost everything with which he came into contact to the scrutiny of his intellect, and formed opinions based upon his own rigorous analysis of things in light of Reason and Revelation. He was rarely, if ever, inclined to brook excuses offered in defense of this or that aspect of the modern world which his own examination found to be damaging to man, whether spiritually or materially. This refusal to compromise; this integrity of vision, of speech, and of action; this radical commitment to the truth, regardless of consequences, earned him, from the influential Catholic philosopher, Frederick Wilhelmsen, the distinguishing label, "No alienated man."

The phrase suggests that Belloc was *not* an "alienated" modern whose religious instinct was suppressed because "God is dead;" whose ability to think and to reason was atrophied because "nothing can be known for certain;" and whose virtue was emasculated for fear of making "offensive value judgments."

No, Belloc possessed a deep religious sense, a ruthlessly logical and coherent mind, and an innate and courageous moral sense. He believed, thought, and acted as an integral Catholic. What further saved him from becoming an "alienated modern" was his honesty – his refusal to lie to himself and to others about modernity, most aspects of which stand condemned in one way or another in the face of evidence presented by the religious, rational, and moral sense.

Belloc's refusal to lie is what made for him so many ideological enemies; yet the same quality makes him for us a beacon of Truth and Sanity in these troubled times. Many are familiar with his academic successes in defending true history against false interpretations, and know well his vigorous defense of Catholicism in the face of its opponents. Those who are fortunate have come across his social criticism contained in such volumes as *The Servile State* and the *Essay on the Restoration of Property*, in which he takes Centralization to task, in both its bureaucratic-socialist *and* its finance-capitalist forms.

Less familiar is his critique of the Press, what we would call a critique of the Media. Though an analysis of the phenomenon of the Media – its growth, its concentration, its impact on public opinion, its ability to suppress truth and warp thinking – *should be* central to any complete conception of "what's wrong with the world," we rarely find a coherent analysis and condemnation of the problem from those who attempt to articulate a vision for the restoration of the West. Richard Weaver is a notable exception; his chapter, "The Great Stereopticon," in *Ideas Have Consequences* is a commendable assessment of the media propaganda machine. Thus it is the comprehensiveness of Belloc's position – from which flows his critique of the Press – that makes *The Free Press* an essential treatise on the corrosive influence exercised by the contemporary media establishment. It is, however, a subtle treatise, and the truly enlightening and remarkable aspects of his work are easily overlooked.

Belloc begins with the rather simple statement that Capitalism and Finance grew out of the Reformation. What he says thereafter, however, is of central importance to his entire essay. The Press, he says, "began to arise contemporaneously with Capitalism and Finance: it has grown with them and served them." Thus Belloc underlines the key to his thought process in a single phrase, a phrase which implies conclusions both shocking and wholly contrary to modern notions.

These notions tell us the following: That the Press, the Media, comprises the Fourth Estate. It shares responsibility for governing the nation, because of the influence it exercises over the voting populace. It therefore considers itself to be a public trust, responsible for bringing accurate and objective news, as well as varied and educated opinion, to the mass of men.

Nothing could be further from the truth, or from Belloc's accurate notion that the Press is the spawn of Capitalism. His idea implies that the modern media corporation exists not to perform a service but rather to make a profit. The so-called "market forces" which govern the workings of the capitalist machine cannot be trusted to ensure that corporations are managed in a way which is beneficial to the average man. Those forces will rather dictate the terms upon which a newspaper (or TV or radio station) succeeds or fails. Those same forces will ultimately cause the independent operation to surrender to the conglomerate or to fold altogether. Thus the only corporations able to sustain an operation for the dissemination of news and opinion – in print or otherwise – will be those with huge amounts of capital. Market forces will finally be quite neutral about *what* is printed or broadcast, unless of course those in a position to influence regulation that is placed upon the market have a vested interest in what is printed or broadcast.

That Belloc's further observations, in illustrating these points – which are focused on the late 19th and early 20th centuries, are not only accurate statements of fact but also prescient warnings about the future, is born out by current evidence. Indeed, each of the implications of Belloc's general thesis corresponds *exactly* to the current situation. Let's look briefly at four of those distinct conclusions.

(1) Profit. It is, of course, naive to expect that altruistic motives will inspire corporations that live and die by profits, including those that belong to the famed "fourth estate." Writing recently on the Press, columnist Molly Ivins said, "Thirty years ago, the publisher of a good-size city daily expected a return of 7 to 8 percent. Today, there is virtually no competition, and getting less than 20 percent is

considered a failure." She continued: "As the ownership of American news media becomes more and more concentrated, with all outlets subject to judgment by some 25-year-old hotshot on Wall Street as to whether they 'meet earnings expectations,' the pressure to cut news gathering gets worse. As far as the media conglomerates are concerned, newspapers and television networks are just 'profit centers'.... If they can make more with a niche-market magazine for knitters, they will. That the media have a public responsibility so important that it is protected by the Constitution gets lost in the profit chase."

Belloc said as much in 1918; his words ring even truer today.

(2) Mergers. According to the "Corporate Accountability Project," in 1983 Ben Bagdikian, author of *The Media Monopoly*, was called "alarmist" for pointing out that "50 corporations controlled the vast majority of all news media in the U.S." Yet in 2000, a mere 17 years later, according to the 6th edition of his book, the number of corporations controlling almost all of America's newspapers, magazines, TV and radio stations, etc., had fallen to six. A Vermont Congressman was recently so annoyed with the situation that, during a U.S. House Financial Services Committee hearing, he confronted the Chairman of the U.S. Federal Reserve over the tendency of corporations – including those in the print and broadcast Media – to consolidate into ever larger corporations, exercising an enormous degree of control over "the United States economy, the people who work for them and the people who purchase their products."

As Belloc points out, the distinction between the capitalists who own the media and the capitalists who advertise with – and thus subsidize – the media is often specious. It would be a mistake to think that Belloc is being merely humorous when he says that "the same man who owned *The Daily Times* was a shareholder in Jones's Soap or Smith's Pills." All of the major media corporations attempt to succeed financially by dabbling in a host of more-or-less related sales and promotional activities designed to sell anything and everything possible based upon their primary mission; Walt Disney, for instance, sells junk food in "ESPN Zone/Studio Grill" restaurants in five of America's biggest cities for no other reason than that it is the owner of the ESPN sports cable network.

The owners of the Media conglomerates are not (merely) professional journalists; they are, rather, giants of the corporate world and the "entertainment" industry. General Electric owns NBC; Walt Disney owns Capital Cities/ABC; Viacom owns both CBS and Paramount; Time Warner owns both CNN and America Online; and Rupert Murdoch's News Corporation owns Fox. The problem is set to get even worse. Based upon recent or pending decisions from the U.S. Federal Communications Commission, some media critics are predicting the possible merger of NBC *with* AOL Time Warner, or, if the rules are relaxed even more, the purchase of NBC by Viacom, which already owns CBS! According to a July, 2001, *Village Voice* article, Viacom President Mel Karmazin recently "announced he 'would absolutely love' to purchase his broadcast rival, a deal that would make the world's third largest media conglomerate (2000 revenues: $20 billion) an even more pervasive presence."

(3) Squashing the little guy. What only serious Distributists seem to bear in mind when contemplating merger after merger is that for every corporate buyer – or winner, there is also a corporate seller – or loser. Despite capitalist guarantees that "merger mania" is merely the working out of the free market, no one in his right mind believes that increased "efficiency and quality" would result from having every newspaper in the country owned by the same giant corporation.

An article from a few years back in a local Maine newspaper, *The Ellsworth American*, detailed some of the media-merger transactions which saw numerous local papers and radio stations gobbled up, but to what purpose? "The Seattle Times Co. acquired Maine's largest daily newspaper, the *Portland Press Herald/Maine Sunday Telegram* [along with the] *Kennebec Journal, Morning Sentinel* and *Coastal Journal*.... Clear Channel Communications of San Antonio, Texas, bought six Maine radio stations between Dexter and Bar Harbor for $20 million.... Last year...American Consolidated Media, Inc., of Dallas, bought Courier Publications in Rockland which owned

The Bar Harbor Times, The Camden Herald, the *Capital Weekly* in Augusta, *The Courier-Gazette* in Rockland, the *Ellsworth Weekly, Lincoln County Weekly* in Damariscotta, and *The Republican Journal* in Belfast. The purchase price reportedly exceeded $11 million." Can it really be the "impulse of the free market" towards efficiency and quality that dictates that Maine media outlets should be owned by operations from Texas and Seattle?

The real impact of this consolidation is the elimination of small, family-run, local, *independent* media operations. "Where does this power grab leave the innovative entrepreneur, the small business, the individual talent and the consumer?" asks William Safire on the OpEd pages of – ironically enough – the *New York Times*. The answer is clear. As a recent article in *The Nation* states so well, "Small stations, unable to compete, sell out, and listeners pay the price…It may be good for Wall Street and the price lobbyists inside the beltway, but on Main Street it means mostly trash and boredom."

Belloc alludes to another aspect of the unholy marriage of Capital and the Media. When he says that the major papers "make and unmake" politicians, he is *not* being cynical; he's being honest. What they also do today, for all intents and purposes, is make and unmake laws. A report in 2000 by the Center for Public Integrity revealed that media corporations, since 1993, contributed $75 million to campaigns for candidates for federal office and from the two major political parties. From 1996 to 2000, "the 50 largest media companies and four of their trade associations have spent $111.3 million to lobby Congress and the executive branch." In sum, "The companies that dominate the airwaves and purvey the news in print are little different from any other industry. They spend millions on campaign contributions. They fly lawmakers and regulators around the world on all-expenses-paid junkets. They hire a 'who's who' of former congressional staffers, members, and FCC officials to plead their cases in the nation's capitol. And more often than not, they get what they want, which is why media corporations are widely regarded as the most powerful special interest in Washington."

(4) Quality. Belloc states that both the tendency of advertising to become a subsidy for the news operation, and the mechanical and industrial influence that is characteristic of Capitalism, created an atmosphere in which the newspaper proprietor got into the habit of caring very little about what was printed or advertised – except where said proprietor *intended* to influence what was printed.

There is little more concern for what is printed or broadcast today. Belloc's observation that the capitalist nature of the Press is its defining characteristic could not be more accurate. Profits and quality rarely go hand in hand. Insofar as the media corporations are *in business*, their self-proclaimed status as public servants becomes just so much spin on print and broadcast revenue-generation.

Defenders of Capitalism, and the capitalist nature of the media corporations, tell us that market forces ensure that companies are optimally sized, and that products are of the highest possible quality and the best possible value. The same should hold true for the "products" produced by the media conglomerates. Yet some of the more honest media personalities admit that such is not the case. Walter Cronkite said exactly the opposite at a recent conference: "Our big corporate owners, infected with the greed that marks the end of the 20th Century, stretch constantly for ever increasing profit, condemning quality to the hindmost...compromising journalistic integrity in the mad scramble for ratings and circulation."

Even those charged with ensuring that the media conducts its affairs in a way consistent with the public interest seem awestruck by the alleged regulatory potential of "the market." U.S. Federal Communications Commission director, Michael Powell, came under fire recently before the U.S. Senate Appropriations Committee for failing to make the FCC an effective barrier to excessive media consolidation, and thereby allowing the media to put interest in market share and profit ahead of the public interest. His response was merely to point out that "the use of market forces can be concomitant with the public interest." Coming from Powell, who recently declared that his "religion is the market," his comment is illustrative of the almost religious nature of the modern faith in the "free market." An economic version of "might makes right," the orthodox capitalist vision of corporate mergers and profit-seeking is to assume that if the market allows it, it must be right. It never occurs to the "faithful" that if the market allows it, perhaps it is because those with the opportunity to manipulate the market, and the most to gain from it, simply make it happen, to the detriment of the common man.

***

Belloc's observations about the connection of Capital with the Press are further developed by his later contention – again, deceptively simple – that the Plutocracy that governs England (and today all modern nations) through the "system of professional politics" is supported by the modern press organization. At first glance this is a rather obvious statement. But any serious examination of the major media outlets yields the unavoidable conclusion that there is no opposition, at least in the mainstream media, to the modern, materialist worldview which is prevalent in theory and which is enforced in practice by the pseudo-democratic "New World Order" and an omnipresent U.S. military machine.

Recently, top media critic, Robert W. McChesney, writing in *The Capital Times*, pointed to the overwhelmingly pro-U.S. government bias in coverage of September 11, 2001, and its aftermath, and identified as the root causes of that bias the very same evils which Belloc identifies. He wrote:

> The news coverage since Sept. 11 has been charged with a tidal wave of ideologically laced emotion better suited to a World Wrestling Federation Smackdown than to a nation facing a grave long-term problem, where the types of public policies pursued in the coming months and years could produce results ranging from highly productive to spectacularly disastrous....
>
> This should be no surprise. The range of "expert" analysis has been limited mostly to the military and intelligence communities and their supporters, with their clear self-interest in the expansion of military and police approaches rarely acknowledged and almost never critically examined. Little has been done to address the astonishing ignorance of Americans regarding the U.S. role in the world, the extensive use of terrorism by the United States,

and the history and politics of the Middle East, Palestine and the Islamic world....

The reasons for this flawed coverage can be located in two places: the weaknesses in the manner professional journalism has been practiced in the United States; and the ultimate control of our major news media by a very small number of very large and powerful profit-seeking corporations.

...[T]he largest media corporations are among the primary beneficiaries of neo-liberal globalization, and of the U.S. role as the enforcer of global political etiquette. *For these firms to provide an understanding of the world in which the United States military and Capitalism are not benevolent forces, might be possible, but it is unlikely* (emphasis ours).

"No one should be surprised," says another recent article in *The Nation*, "by the polls showing that close to 90% of Americans are satisfied with the performance of their selected President, or that close to 80% of the citizenry applaud his Administration's seat-of-the-pants management of an undeclared war. After all, most Americans get their information from media that have pledged to give the American people only the President's side of the story. CNN chief Walter Isaacson distributed a memo effectively instructing the network's domestic newscasts to be sugar-coated in order to maintain popular support for the President and his war. Fox News anchors got into a surreal competition to see who could wear the largest American flag lapel pin. Meanwhile, Dan Rather says: 'George Bush is the President...he wants me to line up, just tell me where.'"

The result of this behavior by what Belloc terms the "Official Press" is the complete absence of debate on subjects which need more than ever to be discussed – such as the role of the U.S. in the world (pre- as much as post-9/11) as self-appointed judge and executioner within the context of an at-least-informal world government which classifies as "terrorist" any nation which doesn't feel inclined to accept unquestioningly the superiority of liberal democracy and Capitalism. It is interesting to note that some officials within the U.S. government feel so strongly about the need for international media "orthodoxy" in support of government policy as to have suggested that a Pentagon Office of Strategic Influence be set up to disseminate true and, perhaps, *admittedly false* news items to foreign media services in order to influence international political events.

No commentary on the tendency of the mainstream media to echo the ideology of the most powerful modern nations would be complete without at least a passing mention of the degree to which coverage of Middle East politics is tilted toward Israeli interests. *Media Beat*'s Normon Solomon, a veteran media watchdog, summarizes the situation with brutal honesty: "Whatever the case may be, there's no doubt that journalists generally understand critical words about Israel to be hazardous to careers. 'Rarely since the Second World War has a people been so vilified as the Palestinians,' comments Robert Fisk, a long-time foreign correspondent for the London-based daily *Independent*. 'And rarely has a people been so frequently excused and placated as the Israelis.... Our gutlessness, our refusal to tell the truth, our fear of being slandered as "anti-Semites" – the most loathsome of libels against any journalist – means that we are aiding and abetting terrible deeds in the Middle East.'"

***

What, then, of the Free Press today? To the fearless and independent sources to which Belloc used to turn in order to understand what was really going on in the world, we find an almost exact parallel. Most interesting of Belloc's remarks concerning the "Free Press" in his day are those regarding the various journals written from a variety of ideological standpoints which could still, nevertheless, be used to get an idea of the truth. In his Dedication, he notes that even though the two "Free Press" papers then extant in England (*The New Age* and the *New Witness*) would remedy nearly every evil with a completely opposite approach, still both of them could be counted upon to express accurately the facts of the evil.

The internet, its own potential for evil notwithstanding, has contributed to the creation of a Free Press in our own time that corresponds strikingly to that which Belloc details. Just as he read Charles Maurras' monarchist paper without swallowing the notion that a monarchy would remedy every evil, and Drumont's anti-Jewish paper without conceding that all ill in the world was caused by Jews, so too we can avail ourselves of a number of solid sources without having necessarily to subscribe to their ideological presumptions.

Libertarian journals such as Antiwar.com and the Llewellyn H. Rockwell electronic magazine can be counted upon for convincing arguments and relevant news in opposition to the imperialism of the U.S. and its European allies as they attempt to maintain the liberal democratic and capitalist world; but in their near worship of the Austrian economists and their veneration of the "free market" as the solution to all economic problems, they are, as Belloc says, "talking nonsense."

There are a number of journals on the left which give the lie to "right-wing" politics by speaking out against neo-conservative hypocrisy and defending truly human (and Catholic) positions such as man's right to enjoy an unpolluted environment (of which he is the God-appointed steward), and an economic landscape which does not devour those who are not willing to prostitute themselves completely to "profit" and "the market." These include *CounterPunch*, "the bi-weekly muckraking newsletter edited by Alexander Cockburn and Jeffrey St. Clair," Sam Smith's *Progressive Review*, and others. But in reading them it must be born in mind these are, after all, "sincere liberals" who believe that every lifestyle is acceptable, and that truth, ultimately, cannot be known with certainty. They are thus a good source of solid critique of the modern possessors of military and economic power, but useless in providing any alternative social or cultural vision.

Then again there are any number of nationalist and patriotic newspapers, magazines, and websites which lament the decay of European culture and national identity. These are an excellent source of news and information about the attack upon European civilization coming from the halls of academia, and Parliaments and Congresses, through immigration and other social policies which promote the extinction of local European cultures and traditions. But when they begin to talk of racial purity, the pseudo-scientific lies of Evolution and Socio-biology, and the deification of the State, they are – as Belloc says – "eccentric and even contemptible."

The internet has also enabled the lone crusader – the independent journalist, social critic, or polemicist – to make his views known with a greater and greater degree of circulation. Well-known writers like Joe Sobran, Charley Reese, and Robert Fisk, as well as a host of others, such as Mark Bruzonsky with his *Middle East Realities* and Bob Djurdjevic of *Truth in Media* fame, who manage websites, e-mail newsletters, and on-line discussions of all ideological stripes and shades, now have an opportunity to make their views known to an unprecedented degree. No wonder that the Establishment is screaming evermore insistently about the need for "internet regulation" – though this attack on freedom of expression will be done in the name of stopping "hate crimes," pornography and criminality. Meanwhile, the internet has facilitated to a large extent the wide dissemination of alternative news and opinion, thus skirting the boycott of editors and advertisers from which the Free Press suffered in Belloc's day.

Belloc further predicted that thanks to the efforts of the Free Press "knowledge of our public evils, economic and political, will henceforward spread." It is still spreading. The internet was abuzz with alternative views of what really happened, and what was the real cause of the events of September 11, 2001. Opinions range from the mildly interesting to the wholly unbelievable. But what is certain is that fewer and fewer people accept the CNN-filtered version of things, and that such skepticism makes the powers that be justifiably nervous. Commenting on the release of the alleged videotape of Osama bin Laden last October, which – it was claimed – proved his responsibility for the September 11 events, U.S. Deputy Secretary of Defense Paul Wolfowitz said to CNN's Wolf Blitzer, "I hope people might quit with these wild conspiracy theories that suggest that someone else – and you know they get pretty wild around the world." These "wild conspiracy theories" wouldn't have attracted his attention unless they were being promulgated and read around the world through the modern Free Press.

Without that Free Press it is unlikely that we would have heard that the "ethnic cleansing" of Albanians, used to justify the 1999 NATO bombing of Serbia, was a fabrication, and that, contrary to the tens or hundreds of thousands which were claimed, the actual number of Albanian deaths was about 2200 – most of which were caused naturally and were certainly *not* the result of mass executions. Nor would we have learned, over the years since the Gulf War, that the story of Iraqi soldiers tearing Kuwaiti babies from incubators – a story used to popularize the war on the American home front – was fabricated by a public relations firm and presented to the U.S. Congress by the daughter of the Kuwaiti ambassador to the U.S. Nor would we be hearing much about Robert Stinett's *Day of Deceit*, which suggests – persuasively – that President Roosevelt not only knew about Pearl Harbor in advance but hoped for something of the sort to push America into the war.

Most recently, we are indebted to the Free Press (specifically the courageous Carl Cameron of the usually mainstream Fox News) for bringing to light a story that has been around for a couple of years regarding an apparent espionage operation underway against the U.S. by Israelis in various lines of work from art sales to telecommunications billing and wiretapping. Most papers and news services skipped the story altogether, but the Free Press has been circulating the story faithfully since it was broken by Cameron in December of last year.

But for all these interesting revelations of fact and valid criticisms of mainstream opinion, the Free Press remains merely a resource to be consulted as an alternative to the mechanical similarity and materialist orthodoxy of the mainstream media. It is a patchwork collection of suppressed facts and "politically incorrect" opinions, some valid, and some not. It is a patchwork which must be integrated and rectified by a context and a vision which is imposed from above, and which can only be the fruit of the dual influence of Reason and Revelation.

Thus we have Belloc's warning to appreciate the monarchist, the socialist, the anti-Jewish, and other papers, not for the vision – though internally consistent, if erroneous – which they possess, but for the facts and perspective which they reveal. It is ultimately in Belloc's Catholic mind, already possessed of a complete and coherent view of the world, that the disparate truths announced by the Free Press are reconciled and interpreted.

So, too, must our appreciation for and use of the modern Free Press be tempered by the recognition that it possesses no inherent guarantee that any and all of its facts and opinions are free from error or worthy of belief. We must "test all things; and hold fast that which is good" (1 Thessalonians 5:21). We live in an age of universal skepticism and militant relativism. The Free Press too, with rare exception, is thus tainted with that intellectual disorder and chaos which is the fruit of the modern world's conception of "freedom," understood not as the ability to do Good, and to believe and speak the Truth, but seen rather as a license to do and say anything in pursuit of power, pleasure, and material satisfaction. It is a license which allegedly permits not only the massive consolidation of corporate media powerhouses in the name of the "free" market, but also the suppression of fact and the manufacture of ideological orthodoxy in the name of preserving, at all cost, the "free" world.

The world must rather be made safe not "for democracy" but for the Truth. A truly Free Press, in the best sense of the term, will be free to speak the truth at all times and on all subjects. Ultimately, media outlets of all kinds "must be subjected," as Pope Pius XII wrote in his encyclical on television and radio, "to the sweet yoke of the law of Christ, if they are not to become a source of countless evils, which will be all the more serious in that they will enslave not only the powers of nature but also those of the soul."

That enslavement has largely come upon us, and the genius of Belloc's essay is that he explains the origins and developments of it from the standpoint of his comprehensive view of the world. His analysis is thus uniquely *comprehensible*. The problem of the Press is the problem of modernity, and its development from the Reformation, Capitalism, and Finance is simply one more symptom of the fundamental modern disease.

> The Directors
> IHS Press
> March 22, 2002
> Feasts of the Seven Sorrows of the Blessed Virgin and St. Isidore the Farmer

"[S]eeing that the chief instrument employed by our enemies is the press, which in great part receives from them its inspiration and support, it is important that Catholics should oppose the evil press by a press that is good, for the defense of truth, out of love for religion, and to uphold the rights of the Church.... [I]t is the duty of the faithful efficaciously to support this press – both by refusing or ceasing to favor in any way the evil press; and also directly, by concurring, as far as each one can, in helping it to live and thrive..."

—Pope Leo XIII
October 15, 1890

Dedication

Kings Land,
Shipley, Horsham.
October 14, 1917.

My Dear Orage,[1]

I dedicate this little essay to you not only because *The New Age*[2] (which is your paper) published it in its original form, but much more because you were, I think, the pioneer, in its modern form at any rate, of the Free Press in this country. I well remember the days when one used to write to *The New Age* simply because one knew it to be the only paper in which the truth with regard to our corrupt politics, or indeed with regard to any powerful evil, could be told. That is now some years ago; but even today there is only one other paper in London of which this is true, and that is the *New Witness*.[3] Your paper and that at present edited by Mr. Gilbert Chesterton are the fullest examples of the Free Press we have.

It is significant, I think, that these two papers differ entirely in the philosophies which underlie their conduct and in the social ends at which they aim. In other words, they differ entirely in religion which is the ultimate spring of all political action. There is perhaps no single problem of any importance in private or in public morals which the one would not attempt to solve in a fashion different from, and usually antagonistic to, the other. Yet we discover these two papers with their limited circulation, their lack of advertisement subsidy, their restriction to a comparatively small circle, possessing a power which is not only increasing but has long been quite out of proportion to their numerical status.

Things happen because of words printed in *The New Age* and the *New Witness*. That is less and less true of what I have called the official press. The phenomenon is worth analysing. Its intellectual interest alone will arrest the attention of any future historian. Here is a force numerically quite small, lacking the one great obvious power of our time (which is the power to bribe), rigidly boycotted – so much so that it is hardly known outside the circle of its immediate adherents and quite unknown abroad. Yet this force is doing work – is creating – at a moment when almost everything else is marking time; and the work it is doing grows more and more apparent.

The reason is, of course, the principle which was a commonplace with antiquity, though it was almost forgotten in the last modern generation, that truth has a power of its own. Mere indignation against organized falsehood, mere revolt against it, is creative.

It is the thesis of this little essay, as you will see, that the Free Press will succeed in its main object which is the making of the truth known.

There was a moment, I confess, when I would not have written so hopefully.

Some years ago, especially after I had founded the *Eye Witness*, I was, in the tedium of the effort, half convinced that success could not be obtained. It is a mood which accompanies exile. To produce that mood is the very object of the boycott to which the Free Press is subjected.

But I have lived, in the last five years, to see that this mood was false. It is now clear that steady work in the exposure of what is evil, whatever forces are brought to bear against that exposure, bears fruit. That is the reason I have written the few pages printed here: To convince men that even today one can do something in the way of political reform, and that even today there is room for something of free speech.

I say at the close of these pages that I do not believe the new spirit we have produced will lead to any system of self-government, economic or political. I think the decay has gone too far for that. In this I may be wrong; it is but an opinion with regard to the future. On the other matter I have experience and immediate example before me, and I am certain that the battle for free political discussion is now won. Mere knowledge of our public evils, economic and political, will henceforward spread; and though we must suffer the external consequences of so prolonged a régime of lying, the lies are now known to be lies. True expression, though it should bear no immediate and practical fruit, is at least now guaranteed a measure of freedom, and the coming evils which the State must still endure will at least not be endured in silence. Therefore it was worthwhile fighting.

Very sincerely yours,
H. Belloc.

"No man who has the truth to tell and the power to tell it can long remain hiding it from fear or even from despair without ignominy. To release the truth against whatever odds, even if so doing can no longer help the Commonwealth, is a necessity of the soul."

The Free Press

> *I propose to discuss in what follows the evil of the great modern Capitalist Press, its function in vitiating and misinforming opinion and in putting power into ignoble hands; its correction by the formation of small independent organs, and the probably increasing effect of these last.*

I

ABOUT two hundred years ago a number of things began to appear in Europe which were the fruit of the Renaissance and of the Reformation combined: Two warring twins.

These things appeared first of all in England, because England was the only province of Europe wherein the old Latin tradition ran side by side with the novel effects of Protestantism. But for England the great schism and heresy of the sixteenth century, already dissolving today, would long ago have died. It would have been confined for some few generations to those outer Northern parts of the Continent which had never really digested but had only received in some mechanical fashion the strong meat of Rome. It would have ceased with, or shortly after, the Thirty Years War.

It was the defection of the English Crown, the immense booty rapidly obtained by a few adventurers, like the Cecils and Russells, and a still smaller number of old families, like the Howards,[4] which put England, with all its profound traditions and with all its organic inheritance of the great European thing, upon the side of the

Northern Germanies. It was inevitable, therefore, that in England the fruits should first appear, for here only was there deep soil.

That fruit upon which our modern observation has been most fixed was *Capitalism*.

Capitalism proceeded from England and from the English Reformation; but it was not fully alive until the early eighteenth century. In the nineteenth it matured.

Another cognate fruit was what today we call *Finance*, that is, the domination of the State by private Capitalists who, taking advantage of the necessities of the State, fix an increasing mortgage upon the State and work perpetually for fluidity, anonymity and irresponsibility in their arrangements. It was in England, again, that this began and vigorously began with what I think was the first true "National Debt"; a product contemporary in its origins with industrial Capitalism.

Another was that curious and certainly ephemeral vagary of the human mind which has appeared before now in human history, which is called "Sophistry," and which consists in making up "systems" to explain the world; in contrast with Philosophy which aims at the answering of questions, the solution of problems and the final establishment of the truth.

But most interesting of all just now, though but a minor fruit, is the thing called "The Press." It also began to arise contemporaneously with Capitalism and Finance: it has grown with them and served them. It came to the height of its power at the same modern moment as did they.

Let us consider what exactly it means: then we shall the better understand what its development has been.

II

THE PRESS means (for the purpose of such an examination) the dissemination by frequently and regularly printed sheets (commonly daily sheets) of (1) news and (2) suggested ideas.

These two things are quite distinct in character and should be regarded separately, though they merge in this: that false ideas are suggested by false news and especially by news which is false through suppression.

First, of News:—

News, that is, information with regard to those things which affect us but which are not within our own immediate view, is necessary to the life of the State.

The obvious, the extremely cheap, the *universal* means of propagating it, is by word of mouth.

A man has seen a thing; many men have seen a thing. They testify to that thing, and others who have heard them repeat their testimony. The Press thrust into the midst of this natural system (which is still that upon which all reasonable men act, whenever they can, in matters most nearly concerning them) two novel features, both of them exceedingly corrupting. In the first place, it gave to the printed words a *rapidity of extension* with which repeated spoken words could not compete. In the second place, it gave them a *mechanical similarity* which was the very opposite to the marks of healthy human news.

I would particularly insist upon this last point. It is little understood and it is vital.

If we want to know what to think of a fire which has taken place many miles away, but which affects property of our own, we listen to the accounts of dozens of men. We rapidly and instinctively differentiate between these accounts according to the characters of the witnesses. Equally instinctively, we counter-test these accounts by the inherent probabilities of the situation.

An honest and sober man tells us that the roof of the house fell in. An imaginative fool, who is also a swindler, assures us that he later saw the roof standing. We remember that the roof was of iron girders covered with wood, and draw this conclusion: that the framework still stands, but that the healing fell through in a mass of blazing rubbish. Our common sense and our knowledge of the situation incline us rather to the bad than to the good witness, and we are right. But the Press cannot of its nature give a great number of separate testimonies. These would take too long to collect, and would be too expensive to collect. Still less is it able to deliver the weight of each. It, therefore, presents us, even at its best when the testimony is not tainted, no more than one crude affirmation. This one relation is, as I have said, further propagated unanimously and with extreme rapidity. Instead of an organic impression formed at leisure in the comparison of many human sources, the reader obtains a mechanical one. At the same moment myriads of other men receive this same impression. Their adherence to it corroborates his own. Even therefore when the disseminator of the news, that is, the owner of the newspaper, has no special motive for lying, the message is conveyed in a vitiated and inhuman form. Where he has a motive for lying (as he usually has) his lie can undo any merely spoken or written truth.

If this be true of news and of its vitiation through the Press, it is still truer of opinions and suggested ideas.

Opinions, above all, we judge by the personalities of those who deliver them: by voice, tone, expression and known character. The Press eliminates three-quarters of all by which opinion may be judged. And yet it presents the opinion with the more force. The idea is presented in a sort of impersonal manner that impresses with peculiar power because it bears a sort of detachment, as though it came from some authority too secure and superior to be questioned. It is suddenly communicated to thousands. It goes unchallenged, unless by some accident another controller of such machines will contradict it and can get his contradiction read by the same men as have read the first statement.

These general characters were present in the Press even in its infancy, when each newssheet still covered but a comparatively small circle; when distribution was difficult, and when the audience addressed was also select and in some measure able to criticize whatever was presented to it. But though present they had no great force; for the adventure of a newspaper was limited. The older method of obtaining news was still remembered and used. The regular readers of anything, paper or book, were few, and those few cared much more for the quality of what they read than for its amount. Moreover, they had some means of judging its truth and value.

In this early phase, moreover, the Press was necessarily highly diverse. One man could print and sell profitably a thousand copies of his version of a piece of news, of his opinions, or those of his clique. There were hundreds of other men who, if they took the pains, had the means to set out a rival account and a rival opinion. We shall see how, as Capitalism grew, these safeguards decayed and the bad characters described were increased to their present enormity.

III

SIDE BY SIDE with the development of Capitalism went a change in the Press from its primitive condition to a worse. The development of Capitalism meant that a smaller and yet smaller number of men commanded the means of production and of distribution whereby could be printed and set before a large circle a newssheet fuller than the old model. When distribution first changed with the advent of the railways the difference from the old condition was accentuated, and there arose perhaps one hundred, perhaps two hundred "organs," as they were called, which, in this country and the Lowlands of Scotland, told men what their proprietors chose to tell them, both as to news and as to opinion. The population was still fairly well spread; there were a number of local capitals; distribution was not yet so organized as to permit a paper printed as near as Birmingham, even, to feel the competition of a paper printed in London only 100 miles away. Papers printed as far from London as York, Liverpool or Exeter were the more independent.

Further the mass of men, though there was more intelligent reading (and writing, for that matter) than there is today, had not acquired the habit of daily reading.

It may be doubted whether even today the mass of men (in the sense of the actual majority of adult citizens) have done so. But what I mean is that in the time of which I speak (the earlier part, and a portion of the middle, of the nineteenth century), there was no reading of papers as a regular habit by those who work with their hands. The papers were still in the main written for those who had leisure; those who for the most part had some travel, and those who had a smattering, at least, of the Humanities.

The matter appearing in the newspapers was often *written by* men of less facilities. But the people who wrote them, wrote them under the knowledge that their audience was of the sort I describe. To this day in the healthy remnant of our old State, in the country villages, much of this tradition survives. The country folk in my own neighbourhood can read as well as I can; but they prefer to talk among themselves when they are, at leisure, or, at the most, to seize in a few moments the main items of news about the war; they prefer this, I say, as a habit of mind, to the poring over square yards of printed matter which (especially in the Sunday papers) are now food for their fellows in the town. That is because in the country a man has true neighbours, whereas the towns are a dust of isolated beings, mentally (and often physically) starved.

IV

MEANWHILE, there had appeared in connection with this new institution, "The Press," a certain factor of the utmost importance: Capitalist also in origin, and, therefore, inevitably exhibiting all the poisonous vices of Capitalism as its effect flourished from more to more. This factor was *subsidy through advertisement*.

At first the advertisement was not a subsidy. A man desiring to let a thing be known could let it be known much more widely and immediately through a newspaper than in any other fashion. He paid the newspaper to publish the thing that he wanted known, as that he had a house to let, or wine to sell.

But it was clear that this was bound to lead to the paradoxical state of affairs from which we began to suffer in the later nineteenth century. A paper had for its revenue not only what people paid in order to obtain it, but also what people paid to get their wares or needs known through it. It, therefore, could be profitably produced at a cost greater than its selling price. Advertisement revenue made it possible for a man to print a paper at a cost of 2d.[5] and sell it at 1d.

In the simple and earlier form of advertisement the extent and nature of the circulation was the only thing considered by the advertiser, and the man who printed the newspaper got more and more profit as he extended that circulation by giving more reading matter for a better-looking paper and still selling it further and further below cost price.

When it was discovered how powerful the effect of suggestion upon the readers of advertisements could be, especially over such an audience as our modern great towns provide (a chaos, I repeat, of isolated minds with a lessening personal experience and with a lessening community of tradition), the value of advertising space rapidly rose. It became a more and more tempting venture "to start a newspaper," but at the same time, the development of Capitalism made that venture more and more hazardous. It was more and more of a risky venture to start a new great paper even of a local sort, for the expense got greater and greater, and the loss, if you failed, more and more rapid and serious. Advertisement became more and more the basis of profit, and the giving in one way and another of more and more for 1d or the 1/2d became the chief concern of the now wealthy and wholly capitalistic newspaper proprietor.

Long before the last third of the nineteenth century a newspaper, if it was of large circulation, was everywhere a venture or a property dependent wholly upon its advertisers. It had ceased to consider its public save as a bait for the advertiser. It lived (*in this phase*) entirely on its advertisement columns.

V

LET US HALT at this phase in the development of the thing to consider certain other changes which were on the point of appearance, and why they were on the point of appearance.

In the first place, if advertisement had come to be the stand-by of a newspaper, the Capitalist owning the sheet would necessarily consider his revenue from advertisement before anything else. He was indeed *compelled* to do so unless he had enormous revenues from other sources, and ran his paper as a luxury costing a vast fortune a year. For in this industry the rule is either very great profits or very great and rapid losses – losses at the rate of £100,000 at least in a year where a great daily paper is concerned.

He was compelled then to respect his advertisers as his paymasters. To that extent, therefore, his power of giving true news and of printing sound opinion was limited, even though his own inclinations should lean towards such news and such opinion.

An individual newspaper owner might, for instance, have the greatest possible dislike for the trade in patent medicines. He might object to the swindling of the poor which is the soul of that trade. He might himself have suffered acute physical pain through the imprudent absorption of one of those quack drugs. But he certainly could not print an article against them, nor even an article describing how they were made, without losing a great part of his income,

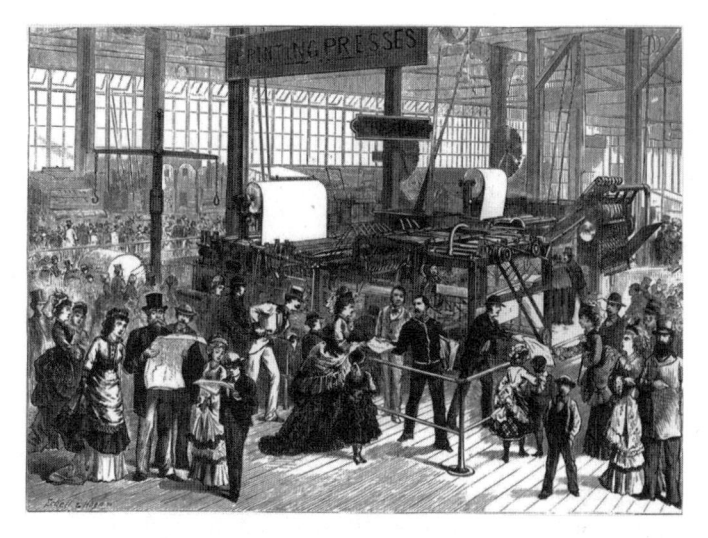

"However bad, shoddy, harmful or even treasonable the matter might be, the proprietor was always at the choice of publishing matter which did not affect him, and saving his fortune, or refusing it and jeopardizing his fortune. He chose the former course."

directly; and, perhaps, indirectly, the whole of it, from the annoyance caused to other advertisers, who would note his independence and fear friction in their own case. He would prefer to retain his income, persuade his readers to buy poison, and remain free (personally) from touching the stuff he recommended for pay.

As with patent medicines so with any other matter whatsoever that was advertised. However bad, shoddy, harmful, or even treasonable the matter might be, the proprietor was always at the choice of publishing matter which did not affect *him*, and saving his fortune, or refusing it and jeopardizing his fortune. He chose the former course.

In the second place, there was an even more serious development. Advertisement having become the stand-by of the newspaper the large advertiser (as Capitalism developed and the controls became fewer and more in touch one with the other) could not but regard his "giving" of an advertisement as something of a favour.

There is always this psychological, or, if you will, artistic element in exchange.

In pure Economics, exchange is exactly balanced by the respective advantages of the exchangers; just as in pure dynamics you have the parallelogram of forces. In the immense complexity of the real world material, friction, and a million other things affect the ideal parallelogram of forces; and in economics other conscious passions besides those of mere avarice affect exchange: there are a million half-conscious and sub-conscious motives at work as well.

The large advertiser still *mainly* paid for advertisement according to circulation, but he also began to be influenced by less direct intentions. He would not advertise in papers which he thought might by their publication of opinion ultimately hurt Capitalism as a whole; still less in those whose opinions might affect his own private fortune adversely. Stupid (like all people given up to gain), he was muddle-headed about the distinction between a large circulation and a circulation small, but appealing to the rich. He would refuse advertisements of luxuries to a paper read by half the wealthier class if he had heard in the National Liberal Club,[6] or some such place, that the paper was "in bad taste."

Not only was there this negative power in the hands of the advertiser, that of refusing the favour or patronage of his advertisements, there was also a positive one, though that only grew up later.

The advertiser came to see that he could actually dictate policy and opinion; and that he had also another most powerful and novel weapon in his hand, which was the *suppression* of news.

We must not exaggerate this element. For one thing the power represented by the great Capitalist Press was a power equal with that of the great advertisers. For another, there was no clear-cut distinction between the Capitalism that owned the newspapers and the Capitalism that advertised. The same man who owned *The Daily Times* was a shareholder in Jones's Soap or Smith's Pills. The man who gambled and lost on *The Howl* was at the same time gambling and winning on a bucket shop advertised in *The Howl*. There was no antagonism of class interest one against the other, and what was more they were of the same kind and breed. The fellow that got rich quick in a newspaper speculation – or ended in jail over it – was exactly the same kind of man as he who bought a peerage out of a "combine" in music halls or cut his throat when his bluff in Indian silver was called. The type is the common modern type. Parliament is full of it, and it runs newspapers only as one of its activities – all of which need the suggestion of advertisement.

The newspaper owner and the advertiser, then, were intermixed. But on the balance the advertizing interest being wider spread was the stronger, and what you got was a sort of imposition, often quite conscious and direct, of advertizing power over the Press; and this was, as I have said, not only negative (that was long obvious) but, at last, positive.

Sometimes there is an open battle between the advertiser and the proprietor, especially when, as is the case with framers of artificial monopolies, both combatants are of a low, cunning and unintelligent type. Minor friction due to the same cause is constantly taking place. Sometimes the victory falls to the newspaper proprietor, more often to the advertiser – never to the public.

So far, we see the growth of the Press marked by these characterisitics. (1) It falls into the hands of a very few rich men, and nearly always men of base origin and capacities. (2) It is, in their hands, a mere commercial enterprise. (3) It is economically supported by advertisers who can in part control it, but these are of the same Capitalist kind, in motive and manner, with the owners of the papers. Their power does not, therefore, clash in the main with that of the owners, but the fact that advertisement makes a paper, has created a standard of printing and paper such that no one – save at a disastrous loss – can issue regularly to large numbers news and opinion which the large Capitalist advertisers disapprove.

There would seem to be for any independent Press no possible economic basis, because the public has been taught to expect for 1d. what it costs 3d. to make – the difference being paid by the advertisement subsidy.

But there is now a graver corruption at work even than this always negative and sometimes positive power of the advertiser.

It is the advent of the great newspaper owner as the true governing power in the political machinery of the State, superior to the officials in the State, nominating ministers and dismissing them, imposing policies, and, in general, usurping sovereignty – all this secretly and without responsibility.

It is the chief political event of our time and is the peculiar mark of this country today. Its full development has come on us suddenly and taken us by surprise in the midst of a terrible war. It was undreamt of but a few years ago. It is already today the capital fact of our whole political system. A Prime Minister is made or deposed by the owner of a group of newspapers, not by popular vote or by any other form of open authority.

No policy is attempted until it is ascertained that the newspaper owner is in favour of it. Few are proffered without first consulting his wishes. Many are directly ordered by him. We are, if we talk in terms of real things (as men do in their private councils at Westminster) mainly governed today, not even by the professional politicians, nor even by those who pay them money, but by whatever owner of a newspaper trust is, for the moment, the most unscrupulous and the most ambitious.

How did such a catastrophe come about? That is what we must inquire into before going further to examine its operations and the possible remedy.

VI

During all this development of the Press there has been present, *first*, as a doctrine plausible and arguable; *next*, as a tradition no longer in touch with reality; *lastly*, as an hypocrisy still pleading truth, a certain definition of the functions of the Press; a doctrine which we must thoroughly grasp before proceeding to the nature of the Press in these our present times.

This doctrine was that the Press was an *organ of opinion* – that is, an expression of the public thought and will.

Why was this doctrine originally what I have called it, "plausible and arguable"? At first sight it would seem to be neither the one nor the other.

A man controlling a newspaper can print any folly or falsehood he likes. *He* is the dictator: not his public. *They* only receive.

Yes: but he is limited by his public.

If I am rich enough to set up a big rotary printing press and print in a million copies of a daily paper the *news* that the Pope has become a Methodist, or the *opinion* that tin-tacks make a very good breakfast food, my newspaper containing such news and such an opinion would obviously not touch the general thought and will at all. No one, outside the small Catholic minority, wants to hear about the Pope; and no one, Catholic or Muslim, will believe that he has become a Methodist. No one alive will consent to eat tin-tacks. A paper printing stuff like that is free to do so, the proprietor could certainly get his employees, or most of them, to write as he told them. But his paper would stop selling.

It is perfectly clear that the Press in inself simply represents the news which its owners desire to print and the opinions which they desire to propagate; and this argument against the Press has always been used by those who are opposed to its influence at any moment.

But there is no smoke without fire, and the element of truth in the legend that the Press "represents" opinion lies in this, that there is a *limit* of outrageous contradiction to known truths beyond which it cannot go without heavy financial loss through failure of circulation, which is synonymous with failure of power. When people talked of the newspaper onwers as "representing public opinion" there was a shadow of reality in such talk, absurd as it seems to us today. Though the doctrine that newspapers are "organs of public opinion" was (like most nineteenth century so-called "Liberal" doctrines) falsely stated and hypocritical, it had that element of truth about it – at least, in the earlier phase of newspaper development. There is even a certain savour of truth hanging about it to this day.

Newspapers are only offered for sale; the purchase of them is not (as yet) compulsorily enforced. A newspaper can, therefore, never succeed unless it prints news in which people are interested and on the nature of which they can be taken in. A newspaper can manufacture interest, but there are certain broad currents in human affairs which neither a newspaper proprietor nor any other human being can control. If England is at war no newspaper can boycott war news and live. If London was devastated by an earthquake no advertising power in the Insurance Companies nor any private interest of newspaper owners in real estate could prevent the thing "getting into the newspapers."

Indeed, until quite lately – say, until about the '80s or so – most news printed was really news about things which people wanted to understand. However garbled or truncated or falsified, it at least dealt with interesting matters which the newspaper proprietors had not started as a hare of their own, and which the public, as a whole, was determined to hear something about. Even today, apart from the war, there is a large element of this.

There was (and is) a further check upon the artificiality of the news side of the Press; which is that Reality always comes into its own at last.

You cannot, beyond a certain limit of time, burke reality.

In a word, the Press must always largely deal with what are called "living issues." It can *boycott* very successfully, and does so, with complete power. But it cannot artificially create unlimitedly the objects of "news."

There is, then, this much truth in the old figment of the Press being "an organ of opinion," that it must in some degree (and that a large degree) present real matter for observation and debate. It can and does select. It can and does garble. But it has to do this always within certain limitations.

These limitations have, I think, already been reached; but that is a matter which I argue more fully later on.

VII

As to opinion, you have the same limitations. If opinion can be once launched in spite of, or during the indifference of, the Press (and it is a big "if"); if there is no machinery for actually suppressing the mere statement of a doctrine clearly important to its readers – then the Press is bound sooner or later to deal with such doctrine: just as it is bound to deal with really vital news.

Here, again, we are dealing with something very different indeed from that title "An organ of opinion" to which the large newspaper has in the past pretended. But I am arguing for the truth that the Press – in the sense of the great Capitalist newspapers – cannot be wholly divorced from opinion.

We have had three great examples of this in our own time in England. Two proceeded from the small wealthy class, and one from the mass of the people.

The two proceeding from the small wealthy classes were the Fabian movement[7] and the movement for Women's Suffrage. The one proceeding from the populace was the sudden, brief (and rapidly suppressed) insurrection of the working classes against their masters in the matter of Chinese Labour in South Africa.[8]

The Fabian movement, which was a drawing-room movement, compelled the discussion in the Press of Socialism, for and against. Although every effort was made to boycott the Socialist contention in the Press, the Fabians were at last strong enough to compel its discussion, and they have by now canalized the whole thing into the direction of their "Servile State." I myself am no more than middle-aged, but I can remember the time when popular newspapers such as *The Star*[9] openly printed arguments in favour of Collectivism, and though today those arguments are never heard in the Press – largely because the Fabian Society has itself abandoned Collectivism in favour of forced labour – yet we may be certain that a Capitalist paper would not have discussed them at all, still less have supported them, unless it had been compelled. The newspapers simply *could* not ignore Socialism at a time when Socialism still commanded a really strong body of opinion among the wealthy.

It was the same with the Suffrage for Women, which cry a clique of wealthy ladies got up in London. I have never myself quite understood why these wealthy ladies wanted such an absurdity as the modern franchise, or why they so blindly hated the Christian institution of the Family. I suppose it was some perversion. But, anyhow, they displayed great sincerity, enthusiasm and devotion, suffering many things for their cause, and acting in the only way which is at all practical in our plutocracy – to wit, by making their fellow-rich exceedingly uncomfortable. You may say that no one newspaper took up the cause, but, at least, it was not boycotted. It was actively discussed.

The little flash in the pan of Chinese Labour was, I think, even more remarkable. The Press not only had word from the twin Party Machines (with which it was then allied for the purposes of power) to boycott the Chinese Labour agitation rigidly, but it was manifestly to the interest of all the Capitalist Newspaper Proprietors to boycott it, and boycott it they did – as long as they could. But it was too much for them. They were swept off their feet. There were great meetings in the North country which almost approached the dignity of popular action, and the Press at last not only took up the question for discussion, but apparently permitted itself a certain timid support.

"Once let the public know what sort of mediocrities the politicians are and they lose power. Once let them lose power and their hidden masters lose power."

My point is, then, that the idea of the Press as "an organ of public opinion," that is, "an expressioin of the general thought and will," is not *only* hypocritical, though it is *mainly* so. There is still something in the claim. A generation ago there was more, and a couple of generations ago there was more still.

Even today, if a large paper went right against the national will in the matter of the present war it would be ruined, and papers which supported in 1914 the Cabinet intrigue to abandon our Allies at the beginning of the war have long since been compelled to eat their words.

For the strength of a newspaper owner lies in his power to deceive the public and to withhold or to publish at will hidden things: his power in this terrifies the professional politicians who hold nominal authority: in a word, the newspaper owner controls the professional politician because he can and does blackmail the professional politician, especially upon his private life. But if he does not command a large public this power to blackmail does not exist; and he can only command a large public – that is, a large circulation – by interesting that public and even by flattering it that it has its opinions reflected – not created – for it.

The power of the Press is not a direct and open power. It depends upon a trick of deception; and no trick of deception works if the trickster passes a certain degree of cynicism.

We must, therefore, guard ourselves against the conception that the great modern Capitalist Press is *merely* a channel for the propagation of such news as may suit its proprietors, or of such opinions as they hold or desire to see held. Such a judgement would be fanatical, and therefore worthless.

Our interest is in the *degree* to which news can be suppressed or garbled, particular discussion of interest to the commonweal suppressed, spontaneous opinion boycotted, and artificial opinion produced.

VIII

I SAY that our interest lies in the question of degree. It always does. The philosopher said: "All things are a matter of degree, and who shall establish degree?" But I think we are agreed – and by "we" I mean all educated men with some knowledge of the world around us – that the degree to which the suppression of truth, the propagation of falsehood, the artificial creation of opinion, and the boycott of inconvenient doctrine have reached in the great Capitalist Press for some time past in England, is at least dangerously high.

There is no one in public life but could give dozens of examples from his own experience of perfectly sensible letters to the Press, citing irrefutable testimony upon matters of the first importance, being refused publicity. Within the guild of journalists, there is not a man who could not give you a hundred examples of deliberate suppression and deliberate falsehood by his employers both as regards news important to the nation and as regards great bodies of opinion.

Equally significant with the mere vast numerical accumulation of such instances is their quality.

Let me give a few examples. No straightforward, common-sense, *real* description of any professional politician – his manners, capacities, way of speaking, intelligence – ever appears today in any of the great papers. We never have anything within a thousand miles of what men who meet them *say*.

We are, indeed, long past the time when the professional politicians were treated as revered beings of whom an inept ritual description had to be given. But the substitute has only been a putting of them into the limelight in another and more grotesque fashion, far less dignified and quite equally false.

We cannot even say that the professional politicians are still made to "fill the stage." That metaphor is false, because upon a stage the audience knows that it is all play-acting, and actually *sees* the figures.

Let any man of reasonable competence soberly and simply describe the scene in the House of Commons when some one of the ordinary professional politicians is speaking.

It would not be an exciting description. The truth here would not be a violent or dangerous truth. Let him but write soberly and with truth. Let him write it as private letters are daily written in dozens about such folk, or as private conversation runs among those who know them, and who have no reason to exaggerate their importance, but see them as they are. Such descriptions would never be printed! The few owners of the Press will not turn off the lime-light and make a brief, accurate statement about these mediocrities, because their power to govern depends upon keeping in the limelight the men whom they control.

Once let the public know what sort of mediocrities the politicians are and they lose power. Once let them lose power and their hidden masters lose power.

Take a larger instance: the middle and upper classes are never allowed by any chance to hear in time the dispute which leads to a strike or a lock-out.

Here is an example of news which is of the utmost possible importance to the commonwealth, and to each of us individually. To understand *why* a vast domestic dispute has arisen is the very first necessity for a sound civic judgement. But we never get it. The event always comes upon us with violence and is always completely mis-understood – because the Press has boycotted the men's claims.

I talked to dozens of people in my own station of life – that is, of the professional middle classes – about the great building lock-out which coincided with the outbreak of the War. *I did not find a single one who knew that it was a lock-out at all!* The few who did at least know the difference between a strike and a lock-out, *all* thought it was a strike!

Let no one say that the disgusting falsehoods spread by the Press in this respect were of no effect. The men themselves gave in, and their perfectly just demands were defeated, mainly because middle class opinion *and a great deal of proletarian opinion as well* had been led to believe that the builders cessation of labour was a *strike* due to their own initiative against existing conditions, and thought the operation of such an initiative immoral in time of war. They did not know the plain truth that the provocation was the masters, and that the men were turned out of employment, that is deprived of access to the Capitalist stores of food and all other necessaries, wantonly and avariciously by the masters. The Press would not print that enormous truth.

I will give another general example.

The whole of England was concerned during the second year of the War with the first rise in the price of food. There was no man so rich but he had noticed it in his household books, and for nine families out of ten it was the one preoccupation of the moment. I do not say the great newspapers did not deal with it, but *how* did they deal with it? With a mass of advocacy in favour of this professional politician or that; with a mass of unco-ordinated advices; and, above all, with a mass of nonsense about the immense earnings of the proletariat. The whole thing was really and deliberately side-tracked for months until, by the mere force of things, it compelled attention. Each of us is a witness to this. We have all seen it. Every single reader of these lines knows that my indictment is true. Not a journalist of the hundreds who were writing the falsehood or the rubbish at the dictation of his employer but had felt the strain upon the little weekly cheque which was his *own* wage. Yet this enormous national thing was at first not dealt with at all in the Press, and, when dealt with, was falsified out of recognition.

I could give any number of other, and, perhaps, minor instances as the times go (but still enormous instances as older morals went) of the same thing. They have shown the incapacity and falsehood of the great capitalist newspapers during these few months of white hot crisis in the fate of England.

This is not a querulous complaint against evils that are human and necessary, and therefore always present. I detest such waste of energy, and I agree with all my heart in the statement recently made by the Editor of *The New Age* that in moments such as these, when any waste is inexcusable, sterile complaint is the *worst* of waste. But my complaint here is not sterile. It is fruitful. This Capitalist Press has come at last to warp all judgement. The tiny oligarchy which controls it is irresponsible and feels itself immune. It has come to believe that it can suppress any truth and suggest any falsehood. It governs, and governs abominably: and it is governing thus in the midst of a war for life.

"For the strength of a newspaper owner lies in his power to deceive the public and to withhold or to publish at will hidden things: his power in this terrifies the professional politicians who hold nominal authority: in a word, the newspaper owner controls the professional politician because he can and does blackmail the professional politician, especially upon his private life."

IX

I say that the few newspaper controllers govern; and govern abominably. I am right. But they only do so, as do all new powers, by at once alliance with, and treason against, the old: witness Harmsworth[10] and the politicians. The new governing Press is an oligarchy which still works "in with" the just-less-new parliamentary oligarchy.

This connection has developed in the great Capitalist papers a certain character which can be best described by the term "Official."

Under certain forms of arbitrary government in Continental Europe ministers once made use of picked and rare newspapers to express their views, and these newspapers came to be called "The Official Press." It was a crude method, and has been long abandoned even by the simpler despotic forms of government. Nothing of that kind exists now, of course, in the deeper corruption of modern Europe – least of all in England.

What has grown up here is a Press organization of support and favour to the system of professional politics which colours the whole of our great Capitalist papers today in England. This gives them so distinct a character of parliamentary falsehood, and that falsehood is so clearly dictated by their connection with executive power that they merit the title "Official."

The régime under which we are now living is that of a Plutocracy which has gradually replaced the old Aristocratic tradition of England. This Plutocracy – a few wealthy interests – in part controls, in part is expressed by, is in part identical with the professional politicians, and it has in the existing Capitalist Press an ally similar to that "Official Press" which continental nations knew in the past. But there is this great difference, that the "Official

Press" of Continental experiments never consisted in more than a few chosen organs the character of which was well known, and the attitude of which contrasted sharply with the rest. But *our* "official Press" (for it is no less) covers the whole field. It has in the region of the great newspapers no competitor; indeed, it has no competitors at all, save that small Free Press, of which I shall speak in a moment, and which is its sole antagonist.

If any one doubts that this adjective "official" can properly be applied to our Capitalist Press today, let him ask himself first what the forces are which govern the nation, and next, whether these forces – that Government or régime – could be better served even under a system of permanent censorship than it is in the great dailies of London and the principal provincial cities.

Is not everything which the régime desires to be suppressed, suppressed? Is not everything which it desires suggested, suggested? And is there any public question which would weaken the régime, and the discussion of which is ever allowed to appear in the great Capitalist journals?

There has not been such a case for at least twenty years. The currrent simulacrum of criticism apparently attacking some portion of the régime, never deals with matters vital to its prestige. On the contrary, it deliberately sidetracks any vital discussion that sincere conviction may have forced upon the public, and spoils the scent with false issues.

One paper, not a little while ago, was clamouring against the excess of lawyers in Government. Its remedy was an opposition to be headed by a lawyer.

Another was very serious upon secret trading with the enemy. It suppressed for months all reference to the astounding instance of that misdemeanour by the connections of a very prominent professional politician early in the war, and refused to comment on the single reference made to this crime in the House of Commons!

Another clamours for the elimination of enemy financial power in the affairs of this country, and yet says not a word upon the auditing of the secret Party Funds!

I say that the big daily papers have now not only those other qualities dangerous to the State which I have described, but that they have become essentially "official," that is, insincere and corrupt in their interested support of that plutocratic complex which, in the decay of aristocracy, governs England. They are as official in this sense as ever were the Court organs of ephemeral Continental experiments. All the vices, all the unreality, and all the peril that goes with the existence of an offical Press is stamped upon the great dailies of our time. They are not independent where Power is concerned. They do not really criticize. They serve a clique whom they should expose, and denounce and betray the generality – that is the State – for whose sake the salaried public servants should be perpetually watched with suspicion and sharply kept in control.

The result is that the mass of Englishmen have ceased to obtain, or even to expect, information upon the way they are governed.

They are beginning to feel a certain uneasiness. They know that their old power of observation over public servants has slipped from them. They suspect that the known gross corruption of the House of Commons is entrenched behind a conspiracy of silence on the part of those very few who have the power to inform them. But, as yet, they have not passed the stage of such suspicion. They have not advanced nearly as far as the discovery of the great newspaper owners and their system. They are still, for the most part, duped.

This transitional state of affairs (for I hope to show that it is only transitional) is a very great evil. It warps and depletes public information. It prevents the just criticism of public servants. Above all, it gives immense and *irresponsible* power to a handful of wealthy men – and especially to the one most wealthy and unscrupulous among them – whose wealth is an accident of speculation, whose origins are repulsive, and whose characters have, as a rule, the weakness and baseness developed by this sort of adventure. There are, among such gutter-snipes, thousands whose luck ends in the native gutter, half a dozen whose luck lands them into millions, one or two at most who, on the top of such a career go crazy with the ambition of the *parvenu* and propose to direct the State. Even when gambling adventurers of this sort are known and responsible (as they are in professional politics) their power is a grave danger. Possessing as the newspaper owners do every power of concealment and, at the same time, no shred of responsibility to any organ of the State, they are a deadly peril. The chief of these men are more powerful today than any Minister. Nay, they do, as I have said (and it is now notorious), make and unmake Ministers, and they may yet in our worst hour decide the national fate.

* * * * *

Now to every human evil of a political sort that has appeared in history (to every evil, that is, affecting the State, and proceeding from the will of man – not from ungovernable natural forces outside man) there comes a term and a reaction.

Here I touch the core of my matter. Side by side with what I have called "the Official Press" in our top-heavy plutocracy there has arisen a certain force for which I have a difficulty in finding a name, but which I will call for lack of a better name "the Free Press."

I might call it the "independent" Press were it not that such a word would connote as yet a little too much power, though I do believe its power to be rising, and though I am confident that it will in the near future change our affairs.

I am not acquainted with any other modern language than French and English, but I read this Free Press French and English, Colonial and American regularly, and it seems to me the chief intellectual phenomenon of our time.

In France and in England, and for all I know elsewhere, there has arisen in protest against the complete corruption and falsehood of the great Capitalist papers a crop of new organs which are in the strictest sense of the word "organs of Opinion." I need not detain English readers with the effect of this upon the Continent. It is already sufficiently noteworthy in England alone, and we shall do well to note it carefully.

The New Age was, I think, the pioneer in the matter. It still maintains a pre-eminent position. I myself founded the *Eye Witness* in the same chapter of ideas (by which I do not mean at all with similar objects of propaganda). Ireland has produced more than one organ of the sort, Scotland one or two. Their number will increase.

With this I pass from the just denunciation of evil to the exposition of what is good.

I propose to examine the nature of that movement which I call "The Free Press," to analyse the disabilities under which it suffers, and to conclude with my conviction that it is, in spite of its disabilities, not only a growing force, but a salutary one, and, in a certain measure, a conquering one. It is to this argument that I shall now ask my readers to direct themselves.

X

THE RISE of what I have called "The Free Press" was due to a reaction against what I have called "The Official Press." But this reaction was not single in motive.

Three distinct moral motives lay behind it and converged upon it. We shall do well to separate and recognize each, because each has had its effect upon the Free Press as a whole, and that Free Press bears the marks of all three most strongly today.

The first motive apparent, coming much earlier than either of the other two, was the motive of (A) *Propaganda*. The second motive was (B) *Indignation against the concealment of Truth*, and the third motive was (C) *Indignation against irresponsible power*: the sense of oppression which an immoral irresponsibility in power breeds among those who are unhappily subject to it.

Let us take each of these in their order.

XI

A

THE MOTIVE of Propaganda (which began to work much the earliest of the three) concerned Religions, and also certain racial enthusiasms or political doctrines which, by their sincerity and readiness to sacrifice, had half the force of Religions.

Men found that the great papers (in their final phase) refused to talk about anything really important in Religion. They dared do nothing but repeat very discreetly the vaguest ethical platitudes. They hardly dared do even that. They took for granted a sort of invertebrate common opinion. They consented to be slightly coloured by the dominating religion of the country in which each paper happened to be printed – and there was an end of it.

Great bodies of men who cared intensely for a definite creed found that expression for it was lacking, even if this creed (as in France) were that of a very large majority in the State. The "organs of opinion" professed a genteel ignorance of that idea which was most widespread, most intense and most formative. Nor could it be otherwise with a Capitalist enterprise whose directing motive was not conversion or even expression, but mere gain. There was nothing to distinguish a large daily newspaper owned by a Jew from one owned by an Agnostic or a Catholic. Necessity of expression compelled the creation of a Free Press in connection with this one motive of religion.

Men came across very little of this in England, because England was for long virtually homogenous in religion, and that religion was not enthusiastic during the years in which the Free Press arose. But such a Free Press in defence of religion (the pioneer of all the Free Press) arose in Ireland and in France and elsewhere. It had at first no quarrel with the big official Capitalist Press. It took for granted the anodyne and meaningless remarks on Religion which appeared in the sawdust of the Official Press, but it asserted the necessity of specially emphasizing its particular point of view in its own columns: for religion affects all life.

This same motive of Propaganda later launched other papers in defence of enthusiasms other than strictly religious enthusiasm, and the most important of these was the enthusiasm for Collectivism – Socialism.

A generation ago and more, great numbers of men were persuaded that a solution for the whole complex of social injustice was to be found in what they called "nationalizing the means of production, distribution and exchange." That is, of course, in plain English, putting land, houses and machinery, and stores of food and clothing into the hands of the politicians for control in use and for distribution in consumption.

This creed was held with passionate conviction by men of the highest ability in every country of Europe; and a Socialist Press began to arise, which was everywhere free, and soon in active opposition to the Official Press. Again (of a religious temper in their segregation, conviction and enthusiasm) there began to appear (when the oppressor was mild), the small papers defending the rights of oppressed nationalities.

Religion, then, and cognate enthusiasms were the first breeders of the Free Press.

It is exceedingly important to recognize this, because it has stamped the whole movement with a particular character to which I shall later refer when I come to its disabilities.

The motive of Propaganda, I repeat, was not at first conscious of anything iniquitous in the great Press or Official Press side by side with which it existed. Veuillot,[11] in founding his splendidly fighting newspaper, which had so prodigious an effect in France, felt no particular animosity against the *Debats*,[12] for instance; his particular Catholic enthusiasm recognized itself as exceptional and was content to accept the humble or, at any rate, inferior position, which admitted eccentricity connotes. "Later," these founders of the Free Press seemed to say, "we may convert the mass to our views, but, for the moment, we are admittedly a clique: an exceptional body with the penalties attaching to such." They said this although the whole life of France is at least as Catholic as the life of Great Britain is Plutocratic, or the life of Switzerland Democratic. And they said it because they arose *after* the Capitalist Press (neutral in religion as in every vital thing) had captured the whole field.

The first Propagandists, then, did not stand up to the Official Press as equals. They crept in as inferiors, or rather as open ex-centrics. For Victorian England and Third Empire France falsely proclaimed the "representative" quality of the Official Press.

To the honour of the Socialist movement the Socialist Free Press was the first to stand up as an equal against the giants.

I remember how in my boyhood I was shocked and a little dazed to see references in Socialist sheets such as *Justice* to papers like the *Daily Telegraph*, or the *Times*, with the epiphet "Capitalist"

The Free Press

put after them in brackets. I thought, then, it was the giving of an abnormal epithet to a normal thing; but I now know that these small Socialist free papers were talking the plainest common sense when they specifically emphasized as *Capitalist* the falsehoods and suppressions of their great contemporaries. From the Socialist point of view the leading fact about the insincerity of the great official papers is that this insincerity is Capitalist; just as from a Catholic point of view the leading fact about it was, and is, that it is anti-Catholic.

Though, however, certain of the Socialist Free Papers thus boldy took up a standpoint of moral equality with the others, their attitude was exceptional. Most editors or owners of, most writers upon, the Free Press, in its first beginnings, took the then almost universal point of view that the great papers were innocuous enough and fairly represented general opinion, and were, therefore, not things to be specifically combated.

The great Dailies were thought grey; not wicked – only general and vague. The Free Press in its beginnings did not attack as an enemy. It only timidly claimed to be heard. It *regarded itself* as a "speciality." It was humble. And there went with it a mass of ex-centric stuff.

If one passes in review all the Free Press journals which owed their existence in England and France alone to this motive of Propaganda, one finds many "side shows," as it were, beside the main motives of local or race patriotism, Religion, or Socialist conviction. You have, for instance, up and down Europe, the very powerful and exceedingly well-written anti-Semitic papers, of which Drumont's *Libre Parole* was long the chief. You have the Single-tax papers. You have the Teetotal papers – and, really, it is a wonder that you have not yet also had the Iconoclasts and the Diabolists producing papers. The Rationalist and the Atheist propaganda I reckon among the religious.

We may take it, then, that Propaganda was, in order of time, the first motive of the Free Press and the first cause of its production.

Now from this fact arises a consideration of great importance to our subject. This Propagandist origin of the Free Press stamped

t with a character it still bears, and will continue to
had that effect in correcting, and, perhaps, destroy-
Press, to which I shall later turn.

at the Free Press has had stamped upon it the
arate particularism.

"Sound writing cannot survive in the air of mechanical hypocrisy. They with their enormous modern audiences are the hacks doomed to oblivion. We, under the modern silence, are the inheritors of those who built up the political greatness of England upon a foundation of free speech, and of the prose which it begets."

Wherever I go, my first object, if I wish to find out the truth, is to get hold of the Free Press in France as in England, and even in America. But I know that wherever I get hold of such an organ it will be very strongly coloured with the opinion, or even fanaticism, of some minority. The Free Press, as a whole, if you add it all up and cancel out one exaggerated statement after another, does give you a true view of the state of society in which you live. The Official Press today gives you an absurdly false one everywhere. What a caricature – and what a base, empty caricature – of England or France or Italy you get in the *Times*, or the *Manchester Guardian*, the *Matin*, or the *Tribuna*! No one of them is in any sense general – or really national.

The Free Press gives you the truth; but only in disjointed sections, for it is *disparate* and it is *particularist*: it is marked with isolation – and it is also marked because its origin lay in various and most diverse *propaganda*: because it came later than the official Press of Capitalism, and was, in its origins, but a reaction against it.

B

The second motive, that of indignation against *falsehood*, came to work much later than the motive of propaganda.

Men gradually came to notice that one thing after another of great public interest, sometimes of vital public interest, was deliberately suppressed in the principal great official papers, and that positive falsehoods were increasingly suggested, or stated.

There was more than this. For long the *owner* of a newspaper had for the most part been content to regard it as a revenue-producing thing. The *editor* was supreme in matters of culture and opinion. True, the editor, being revocable and poor, could not pretend to full political power. But it was a sort of dual arrangement which yet modified the power of the vulgar owner.

I myself remember that state of affairs: the editor who was a gentleman and dined out, the proprietor who was a lord and nervous when he met a gentleman. It changed in the nineties of the last century or the late eighties. It had disappeared by the 1900's.

The editor became (and now is) a mere mouthpiece of the proprietor. Editors succeed each other rapidly. Of great papers today the editor's name of the moment is hardly known – but not a Cabinet Minister that could not pass an examination in the life, vices, vulnerability, fortune, investments and favours of the owner. The change was rapidly admitted. It came quickly but thoroughly. At last – like most rapid developments – it exceeded itself.

Men owning the chief newspapers could be heard boasting of their power in public, as an admitted thing; and as this power was recognized, and as it grew with time and experiment, it bred a reaction.

Why should this or that vulgarian (men began to say) exercise (and boast of!) the power to keep the people ignorant upon matters vital to us all? To distort, to lie? The sheer necessity of getting certain truths told, which these powerful but hidden fellows refused to tell, was a force working at high potential and almost compelling the production of Free Papers side by side with the big Official ones. That is why you nearly always find the Free Press directed by men of intelligence and cultivation – of exceptional intelligence and cultivation. And that is where it contrasts most with its opponents.

C

But only a little later than this second motive of indignation against falsehood and acting with equal force (though upon fewer men) was the third motive of *freedom*: of indignation against *arbitrary Power*.

For men who knew the way in which we are governed, and who recognized, especially during the last twenty years, that the great newspaper was coming to be more powerful than the open and responsible (though corrupt) Executive of the country, the position was intolerable.

It is bad enough to be governed by an aristocracy or a monarch whose executive power is dependent upon legend in the mass of the people; it is humiliating enough to be thus governed through a sort of play-acting instead of enjoying the self-government of free men.

It is worse by far to be governed by a clique of Professional Politicians bamboozling the multitude with a pretence of "Democracy."

But it is intolerable that similar power should reside in the hands of obscure nobodies about whom no illusion could possibly exist, whose tyranny is not admitted or public at all, who do not even take the risk of exposing their features, and to whom no responsibility whatever attaches.

The knowledge that this was so provided the third, and, perhaps, the most powerful motive for the creation of a Free Press.

Unfortunately, it could affect only very few men. With the mass even of well-educated and observant men the feeling created by the novel power of the great papers was little more than a vague ill ease. They had a general conception that the owner of a widely circulated popular newspaper could, and did, blackmail the professional politician: make or unmake the professional politician by granting or refusing him the limelight; dispose of Cabinets; nominate absurd Ministers.

But the particular, vivid, concrete instances that specially move men to action were hidden from them. Only a small number of people were acquainted with such particular truths. But that small number knew very well that we were thus in reality governed by men responsible to no one, and hidden from public blame. The determination to be rid of such a secret monopoly of power compelled a reaction: and that reaction was the Free Press.

XII

SUCH BEING the motive powers of the Free Press in all countries, but particularly in France and England, where the evils of the Capitalist (or Official) Press were at their worst, let us next consider the disabilities under which this reaction – the Free Press – suffered.

I think these disabilities lie under four groups.

(1) In the first place, the free journals suffered from the difficulty which all true reformers have, that they have to begin by going against the stream.

(2) In the second place, they suffered from that character of particularism or "crankiness," which was a necessary result of their Propagandist character.

(3) In the third place – and this is most important – they suffered economically. They were unable to present to their readers all that their readers expected at the price. This was because they were refused advertisement subsidy and were boycotted.

(4) In the fourth place, for reasons that will be apparent in a moment, they suffered from lack of information.

To these four main disabilities the Free Press in *this* country added a fifth peculiarly our own; they stood in peril from the arbitrary power of the Political Lawyers.

Let us consider first the main four points. When we have examined them all we shall see against what forces, and in spite of what negative factors, the Free Press has established itself today.

1

I say that in the first place the Free Press, being a reformer, suffered from what all reformers suffer from, to wit, that in their origins they must, by definition, go against the stream.

The official Capitalist Press round about them had already become a habit when the Free Papers appeared. Men had for some time made it a normal thing to read their daily paper; to believe what it told them to be facts, and even in a great measure to accept its opinions. A new voice criticizing by implication, or directly blaming or ridiculing a habit so formed, was necessarily an unpopular voice with the mass of readers, or, if it was not unpopular, that was only because it was negligible.

This first disability, however, under which the Free Press suffered, and still suffers, would not naturally have been of long duration. The remaining three were far graver. For the mere inertia or counter current against which any reformer struggles is soon turned if the reformer (as was the case here) represented a real reaction, and was doing or saying things which the people, had they been as well informed as himself, would have agreed with. With the further disabilities of (2) particularism, (3) poverty, (4) insufficiency (to which I add, in this country, restraint by the political lawyers), it was otherwise.

2

The Particularism of the Free Papers was a grave and permanent weakness which still endures. Any instructed man today who really wants to find out what is going on reads the Free Press; but he is compelled, as I have said, to read the whole of it and piece together the sections if he wishes to discover his true whereabouts. Each particular organ gives him an individual impression, which is ex-centric, often highly ex-centric, to the general impression.

When I want to know, for instance, what is happening in France, I read the Jewish Socialist paper, the *Humanité*[13]; the most violent French Revolutionary papers I can get, such as *La Guerre Sociale*[14]; the Royalist *Action Française*[15]; the anti-Semitic *Libre Parole*[16], and so forth.

If I want to find out what is really happening with regard to Ireland, I not only buy the various small Irish free papers (and they are numerous), but also *The New Age* and the *New Witness*: and so on, all through the questions that are of real and vital interest. But I only get my picture as a composite. The very same truth will be emphasized by different Free Papers for totally different motives.

Take the Marconi case.[17] The big official papers first boycotted it for months, and then told a pack of silly lies in support of the politicians. The Free Press gave one the truth – but its various organs gave the truth for very different reasons and with very different impressions. To some of the Irish papers Marconi was a comic episode "just what one expects of Westminster"; others dreaded it for fear it should lower the value of the Irish-owned Marconi shares. *The New Age* looked at it from quite another point of view than that of the *New Witness*, and the specifically Socialist Free Press pointed it out as no more than an example of what happens under Capitalist Government.

A Mahommedan paper would no doubt have called it a result of the Nazarene religion, and a Thug paper an awful example of what happens when your politicians are not Thugs.

My point is, then, that the Free Press thus starting from so many different particular standpoints has not yet produced a general organ; by which I mean that it has not produced an organ such as would command the agreement of a very great body of men, should that very great body of men be instructed on the real way in which we are governed.

Drumont[18] was very useful for telling one innumerable particular fragments of truth – such as the way in which the Rothschilds[19] cheated the French Government over the death duties in Paris some years ago. Indeed, he alone ultimately compelled those wealthy men to disgorge, and it was a fine piece of work. But when he went on to argue that cheating the revenue was a purely Jewish vice he could never get the mass of people to agree with him, for it was nonsense.

Charles Maurras[20] is one of the most powerful writers living, and when he points out in the *Action Française* that the French Supreme Court committed an illegal action at the close of the Dreyfus case,[21] he is doing useful work, for he is telling the truth on a matter of vital public importance. But when he goes on to say that such a thing would not have occurred under a nominal Monarchy, he is talking nonsense. Anyone with the slightest experience of what the Courts of Law can be under a nominal Monarchy shrugs his shoulders and says that Maurras's action may have excellent results, but that his proposed remedy of setting up one of these modern Kingships in France in the place of the very corrupt Parliament is not convincing.

The *New Republic* in New York vigorously defends Brandeis[22] because Brandeis is a Jew, and the *New Republic* (which I read regularly, and which is invaluable today as an independent instructor on a small rich minority of American opinion) is Jewish in tone. The defence of Brandeis interests me and instructs me. But when the *New*

"A Prime Minister is made or deposed by the owner of a group of newspapers, not by popular vote or by any other form of open authority."

Republic prints pacifist propaganda by Brailsford,[23] or applauds Lane under the name of "Norman Angell,"[24] it is – in my view – eccentric and even contemptible. *New Ireland*[25] helps me to understand the quarrel of the younger men in Ireland with the Irish Parliamentary party – but I must, and do, read the *Freeman*[26] as well.

In a word, the Free Press all over the world, as far as I can read it, suffers from this note of particularity, and, therefore, of isolation and strain. It is not of general appeal.

In connection with this disability you get the fact that the Free Press has come to depend upon individuals, and thus fails to be as yet an institution. It is difficult to see how any of the papers I have named would long survive a loss of their present editorship. There might possibly be one successor; there certainly would not be two; and the result is that the effect of these organs is sporadic and irregular.

In the same connection you have the disability of a restricted audience.

There are some men (and I count myself one) who will read anything, however much they differ from its tone and standpoint, in order to obtain more knowledge. I am not sure that it is a healthy habit. At any rate it is an unusual one. Most men will only read that which, while informing them, takes for granted a philosophy more or less sympathetic with their own. The Free Press, therefore, so long as it springs from many and varied minorities, not only suffers everywhere from an audience restricted in the case of each organ, but from preaching to the converted. It does get hold of a certain outside public which increases slowly, but it captures no great area of public attention at any one time.

3

The third group of disabilities, as I have said, attaches to the economic weakness of the Free Press.

The Free Press is rigorously boycotted by the great advertisers, partly, perhaps, because its small circulation renders them contemptuous (because nearly all of them are of the true wooden-headed "business" type that go in herds and never see for themselves where their goods will find the best market); but much more from frank enmity against the existence of any Free Press at all.

Stupidity, for instance, would account for the great advertisers not advertising articles of luxury in a paper with only a three thousand a week circulation, even if that paper were read from cover to cover by all the rich people in England; but it would not account for absence *in the Free Press alone* of advertisements appearing in every other kind of paper, and in many organs of far smaller circulation than the Free Press papers have.

The boycott is deliberate, and is persistently maintained. The effect is that the Free Press cannot give in space and quality of paper, excellence of distribution, and the rest, what the Official Press can give; for it lacks advertisement subsidy. This is a very grave economic handicap indeed.

In part the Free Press is indirectly supported by a subsidy from its own writers. Men whose writing commands high payment will contribute to the Free Press sometimes for small fees, usually for nothing; but, at any rate, always well below their market prices. But contribution of that kind is always precarious, and, if I may use the word, jerky. Meanwhile, it does not fill a paper. It is true that the level of writing in the Free Press is very much higher than in the Official Press. To compare the Notes in *The New Age*, for instance, with the Notes in the *Spectator* is to discern a contrast like that between one's chosen conversation with equals, and one's forced conversation with commercial travellers in a railway carriage. To read Shaw or Wells or Gilbert or Cecil Chesterton[27] or Quiller Couch[28] or any one of twenty others in the *New Witness* is to be in another world from the sludge and grind of the official weekly. But the boycott is rigid and therefore the supply is intermittent. It is not only a boycott of advertisement: it is a boycott of quotation. Most of the governing class know the Free Press. The vast lower middle class does not yet know that it exists.

The occasional articles in the Free Press have the same mark of high value, but it is not regular: and, meanwhile, hardly one of the Free Papers pays its way.

The difficulty of distribution, which I have mentioned, comes under the same heading, and is another grave handicap.

If a man finds a difficulty in getting some paper to which he is not a regular subscriber, but which he desires to purchase more or less regularly, it drops out of his habits. I myself, who am an assiduous reader of all such matter, have sometimes lost touch with one Free Paper or another for months, on account of a couple of weeks difficulty in getting my copy. I believe this impediment to apply to most of the Free Papers.

4

Fourthly, but also partly economic, there is the impediment the Free Press suffers of imperfect information. It will print truths which the Great Papers studiously conceal, but daily and widespread information on general matters it has great difficulty in obtaining.

Information is obtained either at great expense through private agents, or else by favour through official channels, that is, from the professional politicians. The Official Press makes and unmakes the politicians. Therefore, the politician is careful to keep it informed of truths that are valuable to him, as well as to make it the organ of falsehoods equally valuable.

Most of the official papers, for instance, were informed of the Indian Silver scandal by the culprits themselves in a fashion which forestalled attack. Those who led the attack groped in the dark.

For we must remember that the professional politicians all stand in together when a financial swindle is being carried out. There is no "opposition" in these things. Since it is the very business of the Free Press to expose the falsehood or inanity of the Official Capitalist Press, one may truly say that a great part of the energies of the Free Press is wasted in this "groping in the dark" to which it is condemned. At the same time, the Economic difficulty prevents the Free Press from paying for information difficult to be obtained, and under these twin disabilities it remains heavily handicapped.

The Political Lawyers

We must consider separately, for it is not universal but peculiar to our own society, the heavy disability under which the Free Press suffers in this country from the now unchecked power of the political lawyers.

I have no need to emphasize the power of a Guild when it is once formed, and has behind it strong corporate traditions. It is the principal thesis of *The New Age*, in which this essay first appeared, that national guilds, applied to the whole field of society, would be the saving of it through their inherent strength and vitality.

Such guilds as we still have among us (possessed of a Charter giving them a monopoly, and, therefore, making them in *The New Age* phrase "black-leg proof"[29]) are confined, of course, to the privileged wealthier classes. The two great ones with which we are all familiar are those of the Doctors and of the Lawyers.

What their power is we saw in the sentencing to one of the most terrible punishments known to all civilized Europe – twelve months hard labour – of a man who had exercised his supposed right to give medical advice to a patient who had freely consulted him. The patient happened to die, as she might have died in the hands of a regular Guild doctor. It has been known for patients to die under the hands of regular Guild doctors. But the mishap taking place in the hands of someone who was *not* of the Guild, although the advice had been freely sought and honestly given, the person who infringed the monopoly of the Guild suffered this savage piece of revenge.

But even the Guild of Doctors is not so powerful as that of the Lawyers, *qua* guild alone. Its administrative power makes it far more powerful. The well-to-do are not compelled to employ a doctor, but all are compelled to employ a lawyer at every turn, and that at a cost quite unknown anywhere else in Europe. But this power of the legal guild, *qua* guild, in modern England is supplemented by further administrative and arbitrary powers attached to a selected number of its members.

Now the Lawyers' Guild has latterly become (to its own hurt as it will find) hardly distinguishable from the complex of professional politics.

One need not be in Parliament many days to discover that most laws are made and all revised by members of this Guild. Parliament is, as a drafting body, virtually a Committee of Lawyers who are indifferent to the figment of representation which still clings to the House of Commons.

It should be added that this part of their work is honestly done, that the greatest labour is devoted to it, and that it is only consciously tyrannical or fraudulent when the Legal Guild feels *itself* to be in danger.

But far more important than the legislative power of the Legal Guild (which is now the chief framer of statutory law as it has long been the *salutary* source of common law) is its executive or governing power.

Whether after exposing a political scandal you shall or shall not be subject to the risk of ruin or loss of liberty, and all the exceptionally cruel scheme of modern imprisonment, depends negatively upon the Legal Guild. That is, so long as the lawyers support the politicians you have no redress, and only in case of independent action by the lawyers against the politicians, with whom they have come to be so closely identified, have you any opportunity for discussion and free trial. The old idea of the lawyer on the Bench protecting the subject against the arbitrary power of the executive, of the judge independent of the government, has nearly disappeared.

You may, of course, commit any crime with impunity if the professional politicians among the lawyers refuse to prosecute. But that is only a negative evil. More serious is the positive side of the affair: that you may conversely be put at the *risk* of any penalty if they desire to put you at risk: for the modern secret police being ubiquitous and privileged, their opponent can be decoyed into peril at the will of those who govern, even where the politicians dare not prosecute him for exposing corruption.

Once the citizen has been put at this peril – that is, brought into court before the lawyers – whether it shall lead to his actual ruin or no is again in the hands of members of the legal guild; the judge *may* (it has happened), withstand the politicians (by whom he was made, to whom he often belongs, and upon whom his general position today depends). He *may* stand out, or – as nearly always now – he will identify himself with the political system and act as its mouthpiece.

It is the prevalence of this last attitude which so powerfully affects the position of the Free Press in this country.

When the judge lends himself to the politicians we all know what follows.

The instrument used is that of an accusation of libel, and, in cases where it is desired to establish terror, of criminal libel.

The defence of the man so accused must either be undertaken by a Member of the Legal Guild – in which case the advocate's own future depends upon his supporting the interests of the politicians and so betraying his client – or, if some eccentric undertakes his own defence, the whole power of the Guild will be turned against him under forms of liberty which are no longer even hypocritical. A special juryman, for instance, that should stand out against the political verdict desired would be a marked man. But the point is not worth making, for, as a fact, no juryman ever has stood out lately when a political verdict was ordered.

Even in the case of so glaring an abuse, with which the whole country is now familiar, we must not exaggerate. It would still be impossible for the politicians, for instance, to get a verdict during war in favour of an overt act of treason. But after all, argument of this sort applies to any tyranny, and the power the politicians have and exercise of refusing to prosecute, however clear an act of treason or other grossly unpopular act might be, is equivalent to a power of acquittal.

The lawyers decide in the last resort on the freedom of speech and writing among their fellow citizens, and as their Guild is now unhappily intertwined with the whole machinery of Executive Government, we have in modern England an executive controlling the expression of opinion. It is absolute in a degree unknown, I think, in past society.

Now, it is evident that, of all forms of civic activity, writing upon the Free Press most directly challenges this arbitrary power. There is not an editor responsible for the management of any Free Paper who will not tell you that a thousand times he has had to consider whether it were possible to tell a particular truth, however important that truth might be to the commonwealth. And the fear which restrains him is the fear of destruction which the combination of the professional politician and lawyer holds in its hand. There is not one such editor who could not bear witness to the numerous occasions on which he had, however courageous he might be, to forego the telling of a truth which was of vital value, because its publication would involve the destruction of the paper he precariously controlled.

There is no need to labour all this. The loss of freedom we have gradually suffered is quite familiar to all of us, and it is among the worst of all the mortal symptoms with which our society is affected.

XIII

WHY DO I SAY, then, that in spite of such formidable obstacles, both in its own character and in the resistance it must overcome, the Free Press will probably increase in power, and may, in the long run, transform public opinion?

It is with the argument in favour of this judgement that I will conclude.

My reasons for forming this judgement are based not only upon the observation of others but upon my own experience.

I started the *Eye Witness* (succeeded by the *New Witness* under the editorship of Mr. Cecil Chesterton, who took it over from me some years ago, and now under the editorship of his brother, Mr. Gilbert Chesterton) with the special object of providing a new organ of free expression.

I knew from intimate personal experience exactly how formidable all these obstacles were.

I knew how my own paper could not but appear particular and personal, and could not but suffer from that eccentricity to general opinion of which I have spoken. I had a half-tragic and half-comic experience of the economic difficulty; of the difficulty of obtaining information; of the difficulty in distribution, and all the rest of it. The editor of *The New Age* could provide an exactly similar record. I had experience, and after me Mr. Cecil Chesterton had experience, of the threats levelled by the professional politicians and their modern lawyers against the free expression of truth, and I have no doubt that the editor of *The New Age* could provide similar testimony. As for the Free Press in Ireland, we all know how *that* is dealt with. It is simply suppressed at the will of the police.

In the face of such experience, and in spite of it, I am yet of the deliberate opinion that the Free Press will succeed.

Now let me give my reasons for this audacious conclusion.

XIV

THE FIRST THING to note is that the Free Press is not read perfunctorily, but with close atttention. The audience it has, if small, is an audience which never misses its pronouncements whether it agrees or disagrees with them, and which is absorbed in its opinions, its statements of fact and its arguments. Look narrowly at History and you will find that all great *reforms* have started thus: not through a widespread control acting downwards, but through spontaneous energy, local and intensive, acting upwards.

You cannot say this of the Official Press, for the simple reason that the Official Press is only of real political interest on rare and brief occasions. It is read, of course, by a thousand times more people than those who read the Free Press. But its readers are not gripped by it. They are not, save upon the rare occasions of a particular "scoop" or "boom," *informed* by it, in the old sense of that pregnant word, *informed*:— they are not possessed, filled, changed, moulded to new action.

One of the proofs of this – a curious, a comic, but a most conclusive proof – is the dependence of the great daily papers on the headline. Ninety-nine people out of a hundred retain this and nothing more, because the matter below is but a flaccid expression of the headline.

Now the Headline suggests, of course, a fact (or falsehood) with momentary power. So does the Poster. But the mere fact of dependence on such methods is a proof of the inherent weakness underlying it.

You have, then, at the outset a difference of *quality* in the reading and in the effect of the reading which it is of capital importance to my argument that the reader should note. The Free Press is really read and digested. The Official Press is not. Its scream is heard, but it provides no food for the mind. One does not contrast the exiguity of a pint of nitric acid in an engraver's studio with the hundred gallons of water in the cisterns of his house. No amount of water would bite into the copper. Only the acid does that: and a little of the acid is enough.

XV

Next let it be noted that the Free Press powerfully affects, even when they disagree with it, and most of all when they hate it, the small class through whom in the modern world ideas spread.

There never was a time in European history when the mass of people thought so little for themselves, and depended so much (for the ultimate form of their society) upon the conclusions and vocabulary of a restricted leisured body.

That is a diseased state of affairs. It gives all their power to tiny cliques of well-to-do people. But incidentally it helps the Free Press.

It is a restricted leisured body to which the Free Press appeals. So strict has been the boycott – and still is, though a little weakening – that the editors of, and writers upon, the Free Papers probably underestimate their own effect even now. They are never mentioned in the great daily journals. It is almost a point of honour with the Official Press to turn a phrase upside down, or, if they must quote, to quote in the most roundabout fashion, rather than print in plain black and white the three words *The New Age* or *The New Witness*.

But there are a number of tests which show how deeply the effect of a Free Paper of limited circulation bites in. Here is one apparently superficial test, but a test to which I attach great importance because it is a revelation of how minds work. Certain phrases peculiar to the Free Journals find their way into the writing of all the rest. I could give a number of instances. I will give one: the word "profiteer." It was first used in the columns of *The New Age*, if I am not mistaken. It has gained ground everywhere. This does not mean that the mass of the employees upon daily papers understand what they are talking about when they use the word "profiteer," any more than they understand what they are talking about when they use the words "servile state." They commonly debase the word "profiteer" to mean someone who gets an exceptional profit, just as they use my own *Eye Witness* phrase, "The Servile State," to mean strict regulation of all civic life – an idea twenty miles away from the proper signification of the term. But my point is that the Free Press must have had already a profound effect for its mere vocabulary to have sunk in thus, and to have spread so widely in the face of the rigid boycott to which it is subjected.

XVI

MUCH MORE IMPORTANT than this clearly applicable test of vocabulary is the more general and less measurable test of programmes and news. The programme of the National Guilds, for instance – "Guild Socialism" as *The New Age*, its advocate in this country, has called it – is followed everywhere, and is everywhere considered. Journalists employed by Harmsworth, for instance, use the idea for all it is worth, and they use it more and more, although it is as much as their place is worth to mention *The New Age* in connection with it – as yet. And it is the same, I think, with all the efforts the Free Press has made in the past. The propaganda of Socialism (which, as an idea, was so enormously successful until a few years ago) was, on its journalistic side, almost entirely conducted by Free Papers, most of them of small circulation, and all of them boycotted, even as to their names, by the Official Press. The same is true of my own effort and Mr. Chesterton's on the *New Witness*. The paper was rigidly boycotted and never quoted. But everyone today talks, as I have just said, of "The Servile State," of the "Professional Politician," of the "Secret Party Funds," of the Aliases under which men hide, of the Purchase of Honours, Policies and places in the Government etc., etc.

More than this: one gets to hear of significant manoeuvres, conducted secretly, of course, but showing vividly the weight and effect of the Free Press. One hears of orders given by a politician which prove his fear of the Free Press: of approaches made by this or that Capitalist to obtain control of a free journal; sometimes of a policy initiated, an official document drawn up, a memorandum filed, which proceeded directly from the advice, suggestion, or argument of a Free Paper which no one but its own readers is allowed to hear of, and of whose very existence the suburbs would be sceptical.

Latterly I have noticed something still more significant. The action of the Free Press takes effect sometimes *at once*. It was obvious in the case of the Spanish Jew, Vigo, the German agent. On account of his financial connections all the Official Press had orders to call him French under a false name. One paragraph in the *New Witness* broke down that lie before the week was out.

XVII

NEXT CONSIDER this powerful factor in the business. *The truth confirms itself.*

Half a million people read of a professional politician, for instance, that his oratory has an "electric effect," or that he is "full of personal magnetism," or that he "can sway an audience to tears or laughter at will." A Free Paper telling the truth about him says that he is a dull speaker, full of commonplaces, elderly, smelling strongly of the Chapel, and giving the impression that he is tired out; flogging up sham enthusiasm with stale phrases which the reporters have already learnt to put into shorthand with one conventional outline years ago.†

Well, the false, the ludicrously false picture designed to put this politician in the limelight (as against favours to be rendered), no doubt remains the general impression with most of those 500,000 people. The simple and rather tawdry truth may be but doubtfully accepted by a few hundreds only.

But sooner rather than later a certain small proportion of the 500,000 actually *hear* the politician in question. They hear him speak. They receive a primary and true impression.

If they had not read anything suggesting the truth, it is quite upon the cards that the false suggestion would still have weight with them, in spite of the evidence of their senses. Men are so built that uncontradicted falsehood sufficiently repeated does have that curious power of illusion. A man having heard the speech delivered by the old gentleman, if there were nothing but the Official Press to inform

---

† A friend of mind in the Press Gallery used to represent "I have yet to learn that the Government" by a little twirl, and "What did the right honourable gentleman do, Mr. Speaker? He had the audacity" by two spiral dots.

opinion, might go away saying to himself: "I was not very much impressed, but no doubt that was due to my own weariness. I cannot but believe that the general reputation he bears is well founded. He must be a great orator, for I have always heard him called one."

But a man who has even once seen it stated that this politician was *exactly what he was* will vividly remember that description (which at first hearing he probably thought false); physical experience has confirmed the true statement and made it live. These statements of truth, even when they are quite unimportant, more, of course, when they illuminate matters of grave civic moment, have a cumulative effect.

I am confident, for instance, that at the present time the mass of middle class people are not only acquainted with, but convinced of the truth, that, long before the war, the House of Commons had become a fraud; that its debates did not turn upon matters which really divided opinion, and that even its paltry debating points, the pretence of a true opposition was a falsehood.

This salutary truth had been arrived at, of course, by many other channels. The scandalous arrangement between the Front Benches which forced the Insurance Act[30] down our throats was an eye-opener for the great masses of people. So was the cynical action of the politicians in the matter of Chinese Labour after the Election of 1906. So was the puerile stage play indulged in over things like the Welsh Disestablishment Bill[31] and the Education Bills.

But among the forces which opened people's eyes about the House of Commons, the Free Press played a very great part, though it was never mentioned in the big Official papers, and though not one man in many hundreds of the public ever heard of it. The few who read it were startled into acceptance by the exact correspondence between its statement and observed fact.

The man who tells the truth when his colleagues around him are lying, always enjoys a certain restricted power of prophecy. If there were a general conspiracy to maintain the falsehood that all peers were over six foot high, a man desiring to correct this falsehood would be perfectly safe if he were to say: "I do not know whether the *next* peer you meet will be over six foot or not, but I am pretty safe in prophesying that you will find among the next dozen three or four peers less than six foot high."

If there were a general conspiracy to pretend that people with incomes above the income tax level never cheated one in a bargain, one could not say "on such and such a day you will be cheated in a bargain by such and such a person, whose income will be above the income-tax level," but one could say: "Note the people who swindle you in the next five years, and I will prophesy that some of the number will be people paying income-tax."

This power of prophecy, which is an adjunct of truth telling, I have noticed to affect people very profoundly.

A worthy provincial might have been shocked ten years ago to hear that places in the Upper House of Parliament were regularly bought and sold. He might have indignantly denied it. The Free Press said: "In some short while you will have a glaring instance of a man who is incompetent and obscure, but very rich, appearing as a legislator with permanent hereditary power, transferable to his son after his death. I don't know which the next one will be, but there is bound to be a case of the sort quite soon for the thing goes on continually. You will be puzzled to explain it. The explanation is that the rich man has given a large sum of money to the needy professional politician. Selah."[32]

Our worthy provincial may have heard but an echo of this truth, for it would have had, ten years ago, but few readers. He may not have seen a syllable of it in his daily paper. But things happen. He sees first a great soldier, then a well-advertised politician, not a rich man, but very widely talked about, made peers. The events are normal in each case, and he is not moved. But sooner or later there comes a case in which he has local knowledge. He says to himself: "Why on earth is So-and-So made a peer (or a front bench man, or what not)? Why, in the name of goodness, is this very rich but unknown, and to my knowledge incompetent, man suddenly put into such a position?" Then he remembers what he was told, begins to ask questions, and finds out, of course, that money passed; perhaps, if he is lucky, he finds out which professional politician pouched the money – and even how much he took!

XVIII

THE EFFECTS of the Free Press from all these causes may be compared to the cumulative effect of one of the great offensives of the present war. Each individual blow is neither dramatic nor extensive in effect; there is little movement or none. The map is disappointing. But each blow tells, and *when the end comes* everyone will see suddenly what the cumulative effect was.

There is not a single thing which the Free Papers have earnestly said during the last few years which has not been borne out by events – and sometimes borne out with astonishing rapidity and identity of detail.

It would, perhaps, be superstitious to believe that strong and courageous truth-telling calls down from Heaven, new, unexpected, and vivid examples to support it. But, really, the events of the last few years would almost incline one to that superstition. The Free Press has hardly to point out some political truth which the Official Press has refused to publish, when the stars in their courses seem to fight for that truth. It is thrust into the public gaze by some abnormal accident immediately after! Hardly had Mr. Chesterton and I begun to publish articles on the state of affairs at Westminster when the Marconi men very kindly obliged us.

XIX

BUT THERE IS a last factor in this progressive advance of the Free Press towards success which I think the most important of all. It is the factor of time in the process of human generations.

It is an old tag that the paradox of one age is the commonplace of the next, and that tag is true. It is true, because young men are doubly formed. First, by the reality and freshness of their own experience, and next, by the authority of their elders.

You see the thing in the reputation of poets. For instance, when A is 20, B 40, and C 60, a new poet appears, and is, perhaps, thought an eccentric. "A" cannot help recognizing the new note and admiring it, but he is a little ashamed of what may turn out to be an immature opinion, and he holds his tongue. "B" is too busy in middle life and already too hardened to feel the force of the new note and the authority he has over "A" renders "A" still more doubtful of his own judgement. "C" is frankly contemptuous of the new note. He has sunk into the groove of old age.

Now let twenty years pass, and things will have changed in this fashion. "C" is dead. "B" has grown old, and is of less effect as an authority. "A" is himself in middle age, and is sure of his own taste and not prepared to take that of elders. He has already long expressed his admiration for the new poet, who is, indeed, not a "new poet" any longer, but, perhaps, already an established classic.

We are all witnesses to this phenomenon in the realm of literature. I believe that the same thing goes on with even more force in the realm of political ideas.

Can anyone conceive the men who were just leaving the University five or six years ago returning from the war and still taking the House of Commons seriously? I cannot conceive it. As undergraduates they would already have heard of its breakdown; as young men they knew that the expression of this truth was annoying to their elders, and they always felt when they expressed it — perhaps they enjoyed the feeling — that there was something impertinent and odd, and possibly exaggerated in their attitude. But when they are men between 30 and 40 they will take so simple a truth for granted. There will be no elders for them to fear, and they will be in no doubt upon judgements maturely formed. Unless something like a revolution occurs in the habits and personal constitution of the House of Commons it will by that time be a joke and let us hope already a partly innocuous joke.

With this increasing and cumulative effect of truth-telling, even when the truth is marred or distorted by enthusiasm, all the disabilities under which it has suffered will coincidently weaken. The strongest force of all against people's hearing the truth — the arbitrary power still used by the political lawyers to suppress Free writing — will, I think, weaken.

The Courts, after all, depend largely upon the mass of opinion. Twenty years ago, for instance, an accusation of bribery brought against some professional politician would have been thought a monstrosity, and, however true, would nearly always have given the political lawyers, his colleagues, occasion for violent repression. Today the thing has become so much a commonplace that all appeals to the old illusion would fall flat. The presiding lawyer could not put on an air of shocked incredulity at hearing that such-and-such a Minister had been mixed up in such-and-such a financial scandal. We take such things for granted nowadays.

XX

WHAT I DO DOUBT in the approaching and already apparent success of the Free Press is its power to effect democratic reform.

It will succeed at last in getting the truth told pretty openly and pretty thoroughly. It will break down the barrier between the little governing clique in which the truth is cynically admitted and the bulk of educated men and women who cannot get the truth by word of mouth but depend upon the printed word. We shall, I believe, even within the lifetime of those who have taken part in the struggle, have all the great problems of our time, particularly, the Economic problems, honestly debated. But what I do not see is the avenue whereby the great mass of the people can now be restored to an interest in the way in which they are governed, or even in the re-establishment of their own economic independence.

So far as I can gather from the life around me, the popular appetite for freedom and even for criticism has disappeared. The wage-earner demands sufficient and regular subsistence, including a system of pensions, and, as part of his definition of subsistence and sufficiency, a due portion of leisure. That he demands a property in the means of production, I can see no sign whatever. It may come; but all the evidence is the other way. And as for a general public indignation against corrupt government, there is (below the few in the know who either share the swag or shrug their shoulders) no sign that it will be strong enough to have any effect.

All we can hope to do is, for the moment, negative: in my view, at least. We can undermine the power of the Capitalist Press. We can expose it as we have exposed the Politicians. It is very powerful but very vulnerable – as are all human things that repose on a lie. We may expect, in a delay perhaps as brief as that which was required to pillory, and, therefore, to hamstring the miserable falsehood and ineptitude called the Party System (that is, in some ten years or less), to reduce the Official Press to the same plight. In some ways the danger of failure is less, for our opponent is certainly less well-organized. But beyond that – beyond these limits – we shall not attain. We shall enlighten, and by enlightening, destroy. We shall not provoke public action, for the methods and instincts of corporate civic action have disappeared.

Such a conclusion might seem to imply that the deliberate and continued labour of truth-telling without reward, and always in some peril, is useless; and that those who have for now so many years given their best work freely for the establishment of a Free Press have toiled in vain. I intend no such implication: I intend its very opposite.

I shall myself continue in the future, as I have in the past, to write and publish in that Press without regard to the Boycott in publicity and in advertisement subsidy which is intended to destroy it and to make all our effort of no effect. I shall continue to do so, although I know that in *The New Age*, or the *New Witness*, I have but one reader, where in the *Weekly Dispatch* or the *Times* I should have a thousand.

I shall do so, and the others who continue in like service will do so, *first*, because, though the work is so far negative only, there is (and we all instinctively feel it), a *Vis Medicatrix Naturæ*:[33] merely in weakening an evil you may soon be, you ultimately will surely be, creating a good: *secondly*, because self-respect and honour demand it. No man who has the truth to tell and the power to tell it can long remain hiding it from fear or even from despair without ignominy. To release the truth against whatever odds, even if so doing can no longer help the Commonwealth, is a necessity for the soul.

We have also this last consolation, that those who leave us and attach themselves from fear or greed to the stronger party of dissemblers gradually lose thereby their chance of fame in letters. Sound writing cannot survive in the air of mechanical hypocrisy. They with their enormous modern audiences are the hacks doomed to oblivion. We, under the modern silence, are the inheritors of those who built up the political greatness of England upon a foundation of free speech, and of the prose which it begets. Those who prefer to sell themselves or to be cowed gain, as a rule, not even that ephemeral security for which they betrayed their fellows; meanwhile, they leave to us the only solid and permanent form of political power, which is the gift of mastery through persuasion.

"...I am yet of the deliberate opinion that the Free Press will succeed."

Notes.

1. Alfred Richard Orage (1873–1934). An influential English editor and social thinker. He became an elementary school teacher at Leeds, Yorkshire, in 1893, lectured on Theosophy, and in 1900 helped found the avant-garde Leeds Arts Club. He moved to London in 1906 and became joint editor in 1907 of *The New Age*, and of which from 1909 until 1922 he was the sole editor and dominant spirit. Some years after he resigned from editorship of that journal, Orage began editing another one, the *New English Weekly*, which he continued to do until his death in 1934. T.S. Eliot remarked of him in a November, 1934, memorial issue of the *Weekly*, "What was great about him was not his intelligence, fine as that was, but his honesty and his selflessness."

2. *The New Age*. A leading journal of politics and culture edited by A.R. Orage and published from 1907 to 1922, which supported the doctrine of the National Guildsmen, otherwise known as Guild Socialism.

3. *New Witness*. Weekly political journal founded in 1912; successor to the *Eye Witness*, founded by Belloc in 1911 and edited jointly by him and Cecil Chesterton. Dedicated to exposing corruption in government, it ceased publication in 1912, at which point Chesterton (*vide infra*, note 27) purchased it, renamed it the *New Witness*, and invited his friend, Ada Jones, to become his editorial assistant. When Chesterton enlisted in 1916, his brother, G.K., took over the paper. In 1925 it became *G.K.'s Weekly*, which G.K. continued to edit until his death in 1936.

4. Cecils and Howards. William Cecil (1520–1598), better known as Lord Burghley, was the real power during the reign of Elizabeth I, and was, in the words of Belloc, "a very great political genius." Belloc further called him "the author of Protestant England" and said that it "was under his rule that the seeds were sown of all that later developed into what is now the English political and social system." The Cecil family is still immensely powerful in England. The Howards were and are known as the Duke of

Norfolk, and are semi-royal. Belloc says: "They had a somewhat different character from all the other great English nobles, although the family was not remarkably old, and the reason of this particular character of theirs was that they stood for a younger branch of the Plantagenet family, which was the true blood royal of England." It is worth noting that Anne Boleyn, one of Henry VIII's six wives, was a Howard with all the complications that that brought with it.

5. 2d. Shorthand for two pence in the old British imperial currency.

6. National Liberal Club. Founded in 1882, it is located at Whitehall Place, London, overlooking the Thames. It is a meeting place for all those who regard themselves as Liberals of one kind or another.

7. Fabian movement. A reference to the Fabian Society, an organization founded in 1884 for the purpose of spreading Socialism by stealth and gradualness as opposed to revolutionary means.

8. A reference to the political issue in England regarding the use of cheap Chinese Labor, which came to the attention of the public during the aftermath of the Boer War. Lord Alfred Milner, British Commissioner in South Africa, anxious to push reconstruction rapidly ahead, was approached by the mine owners of the Rand, who argued that, as a result of his quest for speed, there was a terrible shortage of labor, and that they needed to import Chinese coolies to make good the difference. The owners were less forthcoming about how such cheap labor would greatly increase their profits. The British Prime Minister of the Conservative government, Balfour, readily agreed and by 1905 some 47,000 Chinese had been imported. They lived effectively as indentured slaves to the mine owners. News of this caused great outrage amongst the English working class, because they saw that Capitalism was operating on the premise that labor was a commodity to be used wherever and however it was cheapest. They could work out for themselves – already oppressed and living in dire poverty – the probable future. It became a major issue, and the Conservative government fell as a consequence in the 1906 election.

9. *The Star.* A newspaper founded in 1887 by the radical journalist and Irish Nationalist MP, T. P. O'Connor, who edited the paper along with his assistant, H. W. Massingham. Other radicals who worked for *The Star* included George Bernard Shaw, Ernest Belfort Bax, William Clarke, H.

N. Brailsford (*vide infra*, note 23) and Ernest Parke, famous for his reporting on the Jack the Ripper case. *The Star* merged with *The Evening News* in 1960.

10. Alfred Harmsworth (1865–1922). Better known as Lord Northcliffe, he purchased his first newspaper, *The Evening News*, in 1894 and turned in sufficient profit that he went on to found the *Daily Mail* in 1896, which is still one of the major British tabloids. He was, and is, widely regarded as the man who began the dumbing-down of newspaper readerships, by including in his paper innovations such as sports pages, "human interest stories," a women's section, and the large banner headline. He once said, "when I want a peerage I will buy one" – reinforcing the belief of many like Chesterton and Belloc that peers were largely created *by* and *for* money. A man of limited intellect, David Lloyd-George, described Northcliffe as "one of the biggest intriguers and most unscrupulous people in the country."

11. Louis Veuillot (1813–1883). A French Catholic journalist renowned for his talent and fighting spirit. During his early life he was not especially religious, but following a pilgrimage to Rome, he became a burning champion of Catholicism and of its rights in France. He founded a paper called *L'Univers* to promote this campaign, despite the fact that he was offered many lucrative posts to not do so. The paper was virulently attacked not only by free thinkers and the anti-Catholic forces, but also by Catholic liberals of the stamp of Montalembert and Mgr. Dupanloup. The French Government suppressed *L'Univers* in 1860 when it published Pope Pius IX's encyclical, *Nullis Certe*, which not only rejected Napoleon's demand that the Pope voluntarily surrender the Papal States, but rather reasserted the Church's right to temporal sovereignty over them. *L'Univers* was permitted to resume publication in 1867. Daring, dogmatic and consistent, Veuillot fought to the end.

12. *Le Journal de Debats*. French daily newspaper published in Paris, one of the most influential of the nineteenth century. Moderately liberal and generally Republican, the paper was founded in 1789 to report the debates of the National Assembly and ceased publication in 1944.

13. *L'Humanité*. A French Socialist journal founded in 1904 by Jean Jaurés, leader of the French Socialist Party, with Aristide Briand and Rene Viviani. Jaurés intended the paper to represent all shades of French Socialism, hence

the paper's masthead, "Daily Socialist journal."

14. *La Guerre Sociale.* Weekly Socialist newspaper founded in 1905 by the Hervéists, a Socialist, anti-militarist movement founded by Gustave Hervé, and one of the extreme left factions of French Socialism.

15. *L'Action Française.* A "neo-royalist" daily paper founded in 1908 by Charles Maurras (*vide infra*, note 20) and his collaborators, including author Léon Daudet, historian Jacques Bainville, critic Jules Lemaître, and economist Georges Valois. The movement itself, bearing the same name, was founded in 1899 by Maurras along with Henri Vaugeois, a Professor of Philosophy, and Maurice Pujo, a young writer and journalist; in 1900 a daily review also called *L'Action Française* was launched and remained in publication until the First World War.

16. *La Libre Parole.* A weekly paper founded in 1892 by the French journalist and author Edouard Drumont. The paper advertised that it was dedicated "to the defense of Catholic France against Atheists, Republicans, Freemasons and Jews." It is worth bearing in mind that during that period of European history, the notion of "anti-Semitism" did not possess the stigma that it does today. It was regarded as political opposition to Jewish influence in a more or less Catholic society, rather than an irrational racial hatred. It was discussed by both non-Jews *and* Jews. Interestingly, Theodor Herzl – the founder of modern Zionism – wrote in late 1892 in a private letter to Moritz Benedikt: "I do not consider the anti-Semitic movement altogether harmful. It will inhibit the ostentatious flaunting of conspicuous wealth, curb the unscrupulous behavior of Jewish financiers, and contribute in many ways to the education of the Jews.... In that respect we seem to be in agreement." *Vide infra* note 18.

17. Marconi case. An intricate case of Ministerial knowledge of Government intentions, contracts and share dealing by prominent public figures. The affair centered around the government's intention to build a chain of state-owned wireless stations, the decision to award the contract for the work to the Marconi Wireless Telegraph Company, and the purchase and sale – for large profits – of Marconi shares by government officials who were in a position to know the effects that the awarding of the Marconi contract would have on its share price. The scandal erupted in 1912 and ran, violently, for some 18 months; it came to light principally as a result of Belloc's reporting in his paper, the *Eye Witness*. Frances Donaldson in her

comprehensive book, *The Marconi Scandal*, published in 1962, says: "It is difficult to present the facts with clarity and justice because of the mass of material among which one is forced to discriminate." Nevertheless, G.K. Chesterton, 23 years after the close of the case, wrote: "It is the fashion to divide recent history into Pre-War and Post-War conditions. I believe it is almost as essential to divide them into the Pre-Marconi and Post-Marconi days."

18. Edouard Drumont (1844–1917). A highly influential French journalist, who was a leading light in the anti-Jewish movement of the period. The height of his influence was achieved during the Dreyfus Affair, where he brought to light many interesting and previously unmentioned facts. His book, *Jewish France*, published in 1886, and his paper, *La Libre Parole*, were, according to the Columbia University Press Encyclopaedia, "equally brilliant and virulent." Following his death, he was acknowledged, even by many of his enemies, as a journalist, polemicist and stylist of the first order.

19. Rothschilds. A hugely rich Jewish financial family that was founded in the eighteenth century by Mayer Amschel Rothschild. By 1820, the family had become so powerful that the period became, in the words of Werner Sombart, "the age of the Rothschilds." Sombart commented that by mid-century that power had grown exponentially so much so that it was a common dictum that "There is only one power in Europe, and that is Rothschild." The family remain, internationally-speaking, one of the most influential in the world.

20. Charles Maurras (1868–1952). A highly talented journalist who started out with Maurice Barrès, the leading exponent of French Republican Nationalism. In 1899, Maurras founded *L'Action Francaise* (*vide supra*, note 15); Maurras broke with Barrès when his movement began to advocate what he called "Integral Nationalism," which was Maurras's particular vision of monarchist nationalism. He was condemned by the Catholic Church in 1926 along with his movement, though it is widely believed that this was due to political manipulation. He was rehabilitated in 1939, during the reign of Pope Pius XII. Although anti-German, Maurras was an admirer of Mussolini and Franco. He died in a clinic in 1952.

21. Dreyfus case. The controversy that surrounded the conviction for treason of Capt. Alfred Dreyfus (1859-1935), a French general staff officer.

Dreyfus was accused of spying for the Germans based upon the discovery, at the Germany Embassy in Paris, of a handwritten *bordereau* [schedule] listing secret French documents, originally delivered to Major Max von Schwartzkoppen, the German military attaché in Paris. Dreyfus was alleged to be the originator of the *bordereau*, was tried by a French court-martial, and was convicted of treason in 1894. The affair came back to the attention of the public when in 1896 Col. Georges Picquart discovered evidence incriminating Major Ferdinand Esterhazy as the real author of the *bordereau*. In 1898 it was suggested that the evidence against Dreyfus had been forged, and the case was referred to an Appeals Court wherein a new court-martial was ordered. Though the new court-martial found Dreyfus "guilty with extenuating circumstances" and sentenced him to 10 years in prison, President Émile Loubet issued a pardon, and in 1906 the Supreme Court of Appeals exonerated Dreyfus, who was reinstated as a major and decorated with the Legion of Honor. During these years (1898-1906) the case had become a major political issue and was hotly debated by royalist, militarist, and nationalist elements on the one hand, and by republican, socialist, and anticlerical elements on the other.

22. Louis D. Brandeis (1856–1941). The first Jew to be appointed to the U.S. Supreme Court, he served as Supreme Court Justice from 1916–1939. He was active in Zionist affairs during the First World War, having accepted the role of Chairman of the Provisional Executive Committee for General Zionist Affairs. He had a major impact on the American branch of the Zionist movement, drawing to it a number of sympathizers, and improving its organization and finance. He resigned his official position upon joining the Supreme Court. Nevertheless, he worked behind the scenes to influence President Woodrow Wilson to support the Zionist cause. The *New Republic* was founded in 1914 as a weekly progressivist journal, and despite apparent ideological inconsistencies, it was and remains generally loyal to the spirit of its first editor, Herbert Croly, who, in his 1909 book, *The Promise of American Life*, argued for a centrally planned society based upon the "brotherhood of mankind." Brandeis and Croly corresponded occasionally.

23. Henry Noel Brailsford (1873–1958). A radical left wing journalist born into a Wesleyan Methodist family. He joined the Independent Labour Party in 1907, and became the editor of the ILP paper, *New Leader*, in 1922. During his tenure, he employed people like George Bernard Shaw, H.G. Wells and Bertrand Russell. He was ousted from editorship in 1926

by Labour moderates gathered around Ramsey MacDonald. He was involved in the setting up of the "Left Book Club" with Victor Gollancz, and wrote extensively for the *New Statesman*; he also wrote *War of Steel and Gold* in 1914, and *A League of Nations* in 1917.

24. Norman Angell (1872–1967). Born Ralph Lane, he became famous as "Norman Angell," which were his middle names. His journalistic career began on papers such as the *San Francisco Chronicle* and *St. Louis Globe-Democrat*. He became the editor of Lord Northcliffe's *Daily Mail* in 1905, but resigned in 1912 to concentrate on writing and lecturing. During his tenure he became very well known in political and literary circles. He was briefly a British Labour MP from 1929–31, but thereafter concentrated on promoting his internationalist agenda. He became a member of the internationalist body, the Royal Institute of International Affairs, and won the Nobel Prize for Peace in 1933. His most celebrated book was *The Great Illusion*, published in 1910, which was translated into 25 languages.

25. *New Ireland*. An Irish Nationalist weekly review published in Dublin from roughly 1915 to 1922.

26. *Freeman*. Belloc is probably referring to the *Freeman's Journal*, another Irish Nationalist journal, published daily in Dublin from approximately 1913 to 1924. In 1924 it became *The Irish Independent*, a title which still exists today.

27. Cecil Chesterton (1879–1918). The younger brother of G.K. Chesterton, who, upon Cecil's birth is reputed to have said, "Now I shall have an audience." Cecil Chesterton began a long and prolific career as a journalist, editor, and writer by contributing articles to a variety of London weeklies and dailies. Initially attracted to the Socialist critique of Capitalism, he joined the Fabian Society and the Christian Social Union in 1901, and was elected to the Fabian Executive Committee in 1904. He lost his seat in 1907, perhaps as a result of his bizarre efforts to wed Fabian Socialism with Christianity and Toryism. From 1907-1911 he wrote almost exclusively for Orage's *The New Age* (*vide supra*, notes 1 and 2); in 1911 he worked with Belloc on the *Eye Witness* which he transformed into the *New Witness* in 1912 and edited until his death. He converted to Roman Catholicism in 1912 after a Unitarian upbringing and a stint with the Church of England. His books include *Gladstonian Ghosts* (1905), *G. K. Chesterton: A Criticism* (1908), *The Party System* (co-authored with Belloc) (1911), and *A History of*

the United States (1919). Author J. C. Squire said of him that "there was no better arguer, no abler journalist, in England."

28. Sir Arthur Quiller-Couch (1863–1944). A renowned critic, scholar and educational reformer of his day. His expertise was the vital and artistic nature of language, and how to convey meaning to others. His outstanding work, *On the Art of Writing*, published during World War I, was composed of a series of lectures on writing given at Cambridge University in the period 1913–1914. In 1919 he became the editor of the highly influential *Oxford Book of English Verse*. His view of things was encapsulated thus: "It amounts to this – Literature is not a mere Science to be studied; but an Art, to be practised."

29. Black-leg. A worker who crosses picket lines in industrial disputes when once the relevant trades union has officially called a strike

30. Insurance Act. A reference to the 1911 National Insurance Act which was brought into being by David Lloyd-George. It was the first working class contributory system of insurance against illness and unemployment, and it was obligatory for all workers between 16 - 70 years of age. Workers had to pay 4d a week, whilst the employers and the Government paid 3d and 2d per week respectively. The controversy was multi-faceted. For the Socialists, the Bill was unacceptable because they were means tested – meaning that a bureaucrat decided one's benefit once he had full knowledge of all one's income and savings (a humiliating procedure), and also because they believed that the benefits were wholly insufficient. For Belloc and Chesterton, the Bill was unacceptable because it was *obligatory*. They had no fundamental opposition to insurance for working people, but argued that 4d was too much to be taken from a meager wage, especially when 4d in the here and now could be life and death for a family. It was seen merely as a plaster on the festering wound of a degenerate Capitalism.

31. Welsh Disestablishment Bill. Finally passed in 1914, the bill to end the Church of England's status as religion of the State in Wales had been proposed a number of times since 1870. Until that time, the Anglican Church was the "official religion" in spite of the fact that the vast majority of Welsh folk were Nonconformists, and thus anti-Anglican in religion. Implementation of the bill was delayed until 1920, because of the outbreak of the First World War.

32. Selah. A Hebrew word found at the end of verses in the Book of Psalms and the Book of Habbakkuk. It is believed to be a form of musical direction. Probably Belloc is suggesting that just as musical direction is a fixed element, so the corruption being described by the Free Press is equally fixed and unwavering.

33. *Vis Medicatrix Naturæ.* An expression dating back at least to Hippocrates (ca. 460–377 B.C.); "the healing power of nature."